The New Age Urban Transportation Systems

The New Age Urban Transportation Systems

Cases from Asian Economies

Volume I

Sundaravalli Narayanaswami

BEP BUSINESS EXPERT PRESS

The New Age Urban Transportation Systems: Cases from Asian Economies,
Volume I

Copyright © Business Expert Press, LLC, 2019.

First published in 2019 by
Business Expert Press, LLC
222 East 46th Street, New York, NY 10017
www.businessexpertpress.com

ISBN-13: 978-1-94784-305-9 (paperback)
ISBN-13: 978-1-94784-306-6 (e-book)

Business Expert Press Supply and Operations Management Collection

Collection ISSN: 2156-8189 (print)
Collection ISSN: 2156-8200 (electronic)

Cover and interior design by Exeter Premedia Services Private Ltd.,
Chennai, India

First edition: 2019

10 9 8 7 6 5 4 3 2 1

Printed in the United States of America.

Abstract

Urbanization is the most common global phenomenon in recent times which brings upon huge stress in the existing transportation infrastructure systems in cities. Interestingly, urban (transportation) challenges are more significant in developing countries and specifically in fast growing Asian countries. This is due to the fact that land occupation is very dense and social aspirations for growth (and therefore mobility) are much higher in developing countries than in developed countries. Limited urban space and infrastructure fail to meet the rapid and huge demands in traffic volume and better quality of services. Therefore the need for design, development, operations and regulation of modern urban transportation systems is more intense than ever.

Infrastructural development and transportation operations are mainly directed at citizen welfare, and they require huge capital investments. Therefore, in many countries urban transportation projects are initiated and executed by the states. Mostly, states opt for private participation so as to minimize the risks in terms of project design, time planning, consortia participation, and quality of execution. This brings a very interesting caveat to the domain. Per se, there are several commonalities in the planning and management of urban transportation projects across the globe. But the approach and solutions have to be developed specific to a local context and relevance. Urban transportation as a domain, is multi-disciplinary, interdependencies between the components are complex and repeatability (and inter-operability) of developed models or solutions is near impossible. Specific challenges include land use planning based on socio-economic distribution, project designing, implementation, financial analysis, governmental decisions that involve several stakeholders with varied capabilities and roles.

We comprehensively cover the domain background, challenges involved in developing such large scale, capital intensive projects of long gestation period and various approaches adopted by different countries. We substantiate our discussions with five real-life cases on modern urban transportation systems from Asian countries, as an illustration of what works and what does not in a particular context. The book is aimed as a one-point reference on modern day developments on urban transportation for a readership of consultants, practitioners, developers, policy makers, and academicians.

Keywords

bus rapid transit; light rail; metro railways; modern urban transit; urban congestion; urbanization

Contents

Preface

Urbanization is the most common global phenomenon in recent times which brings upon huge stress in the existing infrastructure and transportation systems in cities. Interestingly, urban (transportation) challenges are more significant in developing countries and specifically in fast growing Asian countries. This is due to the fact that land occupation is very dense and social aspirations for growth (and therefore demand for mobility) are much higher in developing countries than in developed countries. Limited urban space and infrastructure fail to meet the rapid and huge demands in traffic volume and better quality of services. Therefore the need for design, development, operations and regulation of modern urban transportation systems is more intense than ever.

Infrastructural development and transportation operations are mainly directed at citizen welfare, and they require huge capital investments. Therefore, in many countries urban transportation projects are initiated and executed by the states. Mostly, states opt for private participation so as to minimize the risks in terms of project design, time planning, consortia participation and quality of execution. This brings a very interesting caveat to the domain. Per se, there are several commonalities in the planning and management of urban transportation projects across the globe. But the approach and solutions have to be developed specific to a local context and relevance. Urban transportation as a domain, is multi-disciplinary, interdependencies between the components are complex and repeatability (and inter-operability) of developed models or solutions is near impossible. Specific challenges include land use planning based on socio-economic distribution, project designing, implementation, financial analysis, governmental decisions that involve several stakeholders with varied capabilities and roles.

We comprehensively cover the domain background, challenges involved in developing such large scale, capital intensive projects of long gestation period and various approaches adopted by different countries. The discussions are presented through five real-life cases on modern urban transportation systems from Asian countries, as an illustration of what works and what does not in a particular context. The cities that are covered in the text are Delhi, Ahmedabad, Pune, Singapore, and Yichang. The text is organized as two volumes; the cases on Delhi, Ahmedabad, and Pune are covered in Volume I and those of Singapore and Yichang are covered in Volume II. The introduction chapter discusses the background of urban transportation planning, specifically related to Asian countries and the challenges involved. This is followed up with a detailed coverage of modern transportation systems in the five Asian cities, each presented as a chapter. The conclusion chapter summarizes the discussion. Brief comparison of the transport systems in five cities along with the interpretations and insights are presented.

Acknowledgments

I would like to acknowledge the research support provided by Divyansh Ameta, Dheeraj Badarala, Moxanki Bhavsar and Abhishikt Chouhan. I thank Harshad Parmar, who helped me very much in documentation and word processing. Sincere acknowledgements are due to Jayashree Rammohan and Nishi Peter for their support with language editing of chapters. Special thanks are due to Roystan La'Porte and Scott Isenberg from the Business Expert Press team. My Institute's role in providing us an ecosystem for research and writing is gratefully acknowledged. Finally, I thank my beautiful family that is ever supportive and appreciative of my work.

CHAPTER 1

Introduction

Urbanization

The recent trend in urban growth all over the world is unprecedented and quite alarming. Recently it has been estimated that around three billion people, amounting to 50 percent of the world population live in urban regions. It was significantly different until, some 30 years ago, when there was an even distribution of population in urban and rural areas. In the future, the situation is projected to grow worse than the current levels of urbanization. In the early 20th century, only 16 cities had more than a million people, whereas today almost 500 cities have a million people or more. Understandably, dynamism in urbanization is more rapid in developing countries than developed countries, as they are the regions of high economic growth and social development. Nearly 350 cities in developing countries contain a population of one million or more. Cities are centers of economic activities that contribute to the national growth and socio-economic development by virtue of increased productivity and huge employment opportunities. Expanding boundaries and increasing population in urban regions impose a huge stress on existing urban services and public utility, major of which are education, health care and employment; mobility choice and urban transport are important components of state jurisdiction that enables managing most of the public services. Specifically, mobility is just not about building infrastructure and making available modern automobiles. A good urban transportation system should be built on bringing people closer to the places, so that services are accessible in an easy manner. There are several dependencies and enablers in providing and managing citizen accessibility.

Figure 1.1 depicts that urban population in developed countries is gradually decreasing since 1970 to 1975 periods, whereas in developing

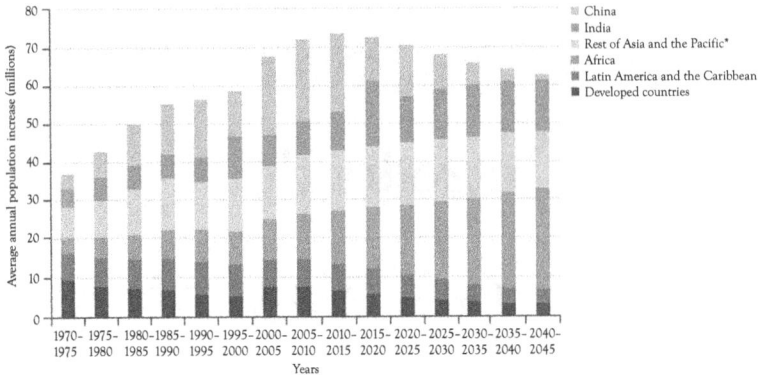

Figure 1.1 *Average urban population increase by region: statistical and projected*

Source: UN-Habitat (2013).

countries, urban population is increasing rapidly. Specifically India will continue to lead the magnitude of increase in urban population and urban population in China is projected to decline in future.

Challenges in Studying Urbanization

The foremost difficulty in studying urbanization is the huge disparity in the definition of urban space; states, provinces and countries define urban area differently. The second challenge is about lack of reliable data related to demography in several countries. The other specific challenges related to mobility and transportation is density of population and topography of urban space. Few (African, South American, and Asian) countries base it on the population size of a locality to classify between urban and rural. However, the difference in population size could be as high as few thousands. There are also countries where both population sizes as well as economic activity are used to distinguish between urban and rural. Botswana considers any region with an agglomeration of more than 5,000 people and more than 75 percent of non-agrarian economic activity as urban and the rest as rural. Urban boundaries are also decided based on governance and administration. At several periods of times, such boundaries kept changing depending on the National Governmental agenda and policies. Specifically, China had a substantial change of defining urban space over time. Lack of reliable demographic data has compounded managing the urbanization challenges. It was also not uncommon to both over- and under-estimate the future population growth. Notwithstanding the fact, that the global population by itself had a steep increase from around 1.6 to 6.1 billion in the past century, and the major share of increase was from developing countries, to be precise, India and China. As of 2017, the global population is 7.5 million, based on the recent UN report (UN Report 2017). Globally, 50 percent population lives in urban space, of which approximately 70 percent are from developing countries and 30 percent in developed countries.

Global Scenario: Urbanization and Impact on Urban Transport

The variances in the basic estimation of urbanization impact urban mobility and transport services. In general states provision transport services all over the world; transport services are owned, operated and managed by the government themselves or they facilitate transport services through a number of private entities. The role of private entities could be formal, informal or a combination of two. The involvement of private entities could be in manufacturing of vehicles (assets related to transport services) and development of infrastructure (design and building) and operations, control and management of transport and allied services. The states, in general, engage private entities, where there is shortage or gap from the state side (Serafeim and Freiberg, 2017) Governmental policies that are subject to different changes from time-to-time have an impact on the role and extent of private involvement in state provisioned services; transport services are one such. Transport services are significant because of the huge investments (funds, effort, and time) required, potential for revenue generation and social benefits such as sustainable environments, therefore contributing to the national economy and pride. As transport services also affect every class of society and therefore the value perception of the citizen needs to be managed.

In Figure 1.2a to 1.2c, the growth of urban areas and decline of rural spaces over few years in India, China, and Singapore are illustrated respectively, along with the corresponding regions they belong to.

Percentage of population in urban and rural areas
India
◆ Urban ◆ Rural

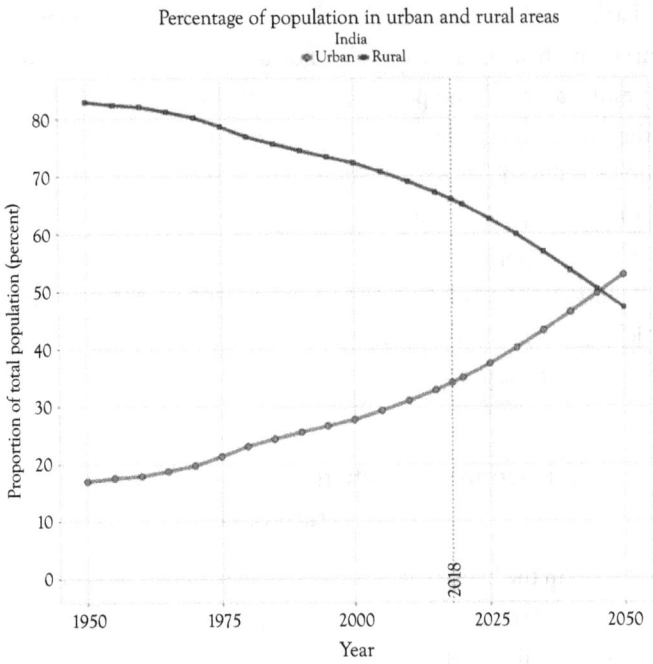

Percentage urban by region and subregion
◆ India ◆ Southern Asia ◆ Asia

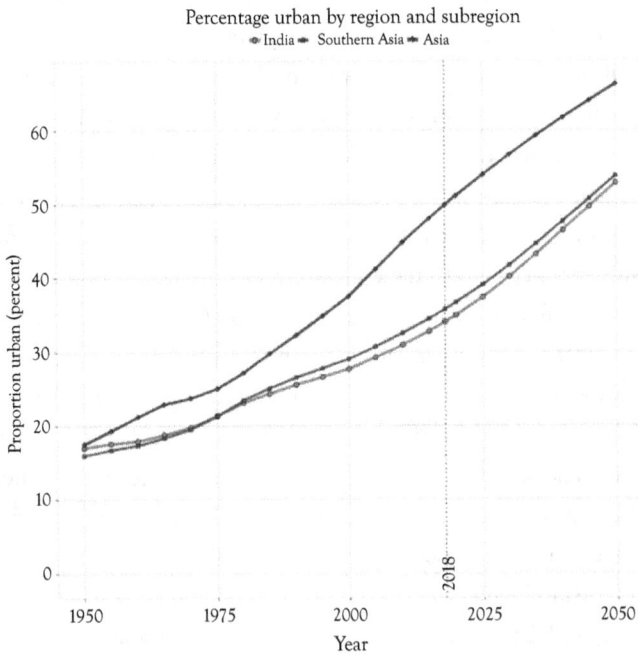

Figure 1.2a Percentage of population change in urban rural areas
(India and South Asia)

Percentage of population in urban and rural areas
China
⬥ Urban ⬥ Rural

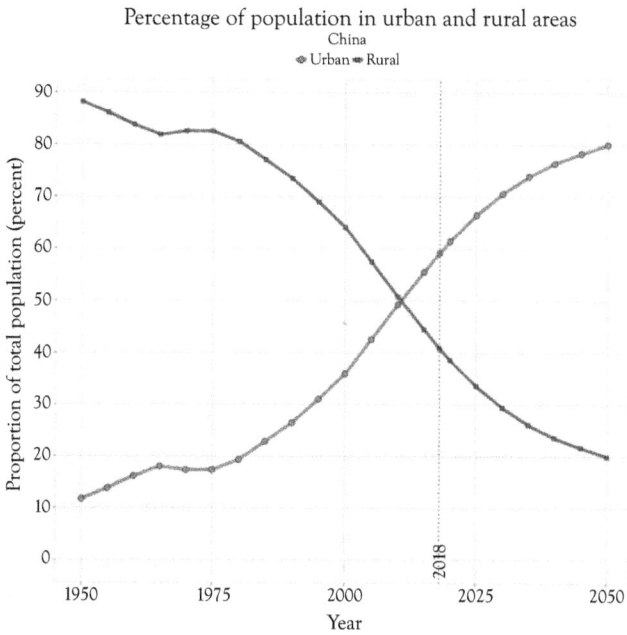

Percentage urban by region and subregion
⬥ China ⬥ Eastern Asia ⬥ Asia

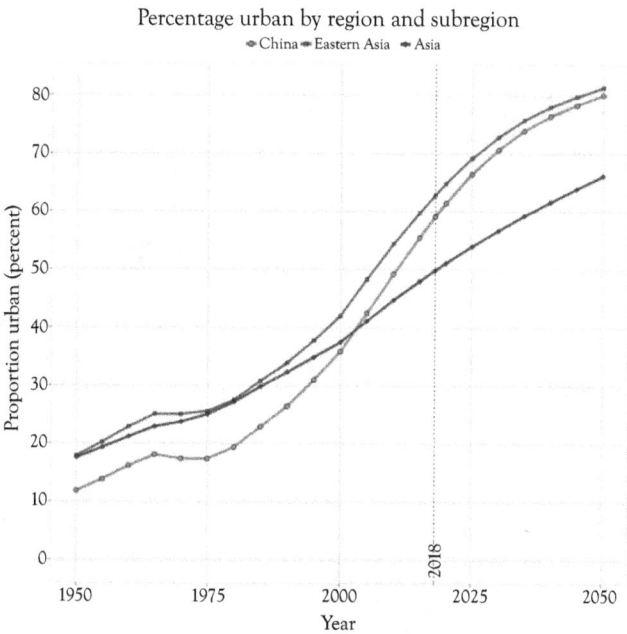

Figure 1.2b Percentage of population change in urban rural areas (India and Eastern Asia)

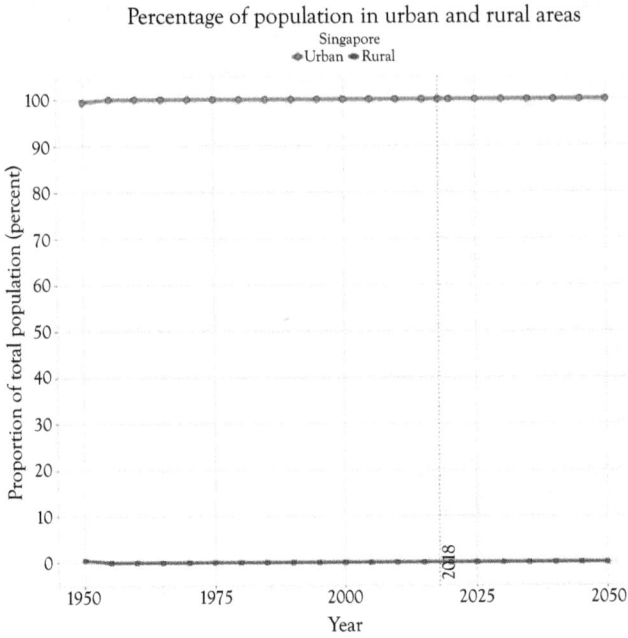

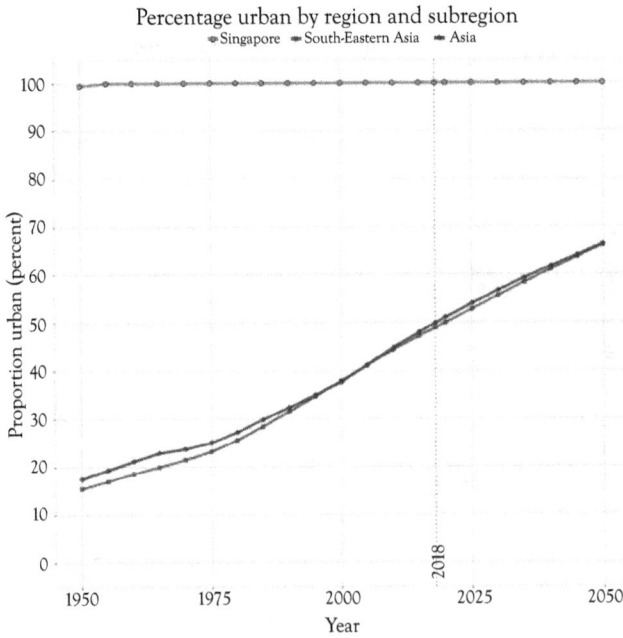

Figure 1.2c *Percentage of population change in urban rural areas (Singapore and South-East Asia)*

Land Usage and Transportation

Motorization

Motorization, the increased usage of vehicles also hugely impacts the urban mobility. Advancement of vehicular technology brings forth modern and high quality vehicles that basically improve the commuter convenience. (Segel and Hartleben, 2015) There are a number of factors that contribute to the increase in number of vehicles on the road. Several cities are ill-planned with no control over where and how rapid land occupancy expands in urban regions of developing countries. As cities grow, land prices increase and agglomeration is more concentrated in the urban periphery, whereas economic and commercial activities predominantly happen at the city centers. Therefore commuting becomes essential. The role of governments in urban development and transport provisioning is also significant. Specifically in developing countries, transportation governing policies do not discourage private vehicle usage and also governments are unable to develop and provide a good public transport service for the growing population. All these factors force people to buy, possess and use private vehicles, as a dependent means of mobility. Non-motorized private transport and unorganized transport modes that are both motorized and non-motorized also proliferate.

One of the major negative impact of motorization, which included two-wheeler and unorganized travel segment is on human safety (Pucher et al. 2007). Road accidents continue to increase both in India and China, as the road is used by multiple vehicles and pedestrians with no dedicated lanes and with weak law enforcement.

Infrastructure Development

Infrastructure development in several countries is less planned and not commensurate with the pace of urban sprawl. Democratically elected governments often pursue a decentralized approach and focus on improving public services and economic infrastructure to sustain growth and inward investment. Two features that are essential, if decentralization is to contribute to economic development irrespective of the substantive democratic dimension: (1) accountability and (2) administrative capacity to implement public policies based on accurate information about local conditions; they are often lacking in several countries as institutional readiness and capability to make financial commitments are missed. Countries like China follow a centralized approach, where the tax revenues and public expenditure are tied to the central and provincial governments. Decentralization helps the governments to break the challenges into smaller manageable problems with better fund realization possibilities, particularly in bigger countries with large population, whereas centralization provides better monitoring and control ability, and therefore infrastructure development projects are better managed, in terms of time, cost, risk and quality.

Sustainability

A macro objective of decentralization is to ensure regional equity with balanced development, based on local strengths (Cohen 2006). To achieve a sustainable urban transportation system, three pillars are vital: (1) a well-coordinated government, (2) good public financing, and (3) fair legislation. Local governance often falls short because the preoccupations and focus of the elected leaders, administrators and civil society organizations are limited to the term-of-office and several vested interests for several sections of society. Sustainability has long-term effects, though investment decisions and investments are needed immediately. There is also little to confirm investments related to sustainability in terms of financial and economic parameters such as Net-present value (NPV) or cost-benefit analysis (CBA) toward various regulatory standards and enforcement bodies. It is crucial that government policies incorporate mechanisms by which robust "macro" long-term strategic plans are approved, developed and implemented in a seamless manner.

Public Transport and Government Policies

Several challenges related to urban transport administration are interconnected and highly complex, as multiple stakeholders are involved. Such issues are generally addressed through government institutions specifically constituted for the purpose. It is required to bring together multiple constituents such as urban and rural municipalities together, coordinate projects, allocate and distribute funds, execute project, and initiate operations to achieve a common objective of efficient land-use planning, public transport and economic development. One of the main reasons for urban congestion arises from the government's inability to provide a quality transport service, in response to the growing demands from an increasing population size. Governments have heavily invested in land usage development, transport infrastructure and service development; however, the pace of urban growth often out passes the rapidity of development. Government policies are also not consistent with the National objectives that change in a short term frame based on elected governments. Most evident is the lack of affordable and convenient public transportation, which is primarily the state's responsibility.

Conclusion

Many countries face severe traffic congestions along with air and noise pollution, road accidents and deteriorating quality of mobility for the poor. Specifically India and China have been experiencing rapid population growth, urban sprawl, sharp increases in motor vehicle ownership and low per-capita income. Both countries have relied on increased motorization to stimulate their economies and also attempted to modernize their transport systems, and to meet the growing demand for cars and motorcycles among the middle and upper classes. An important policy decision needs to be taken on mitigating the negative social and environmental costs of increased motor vehicle use. The most rational and pragmatic solution would be develop good quality, safe, affordable mass transit systems that the people are encouraged to use. The Delhi Metro is a standing testimony in improving the traffic conditions of New Delhi. In summary:

- Transport infrastructure investment and development should be in modern mass transit systems that can cater to high volume of traffic.
- BRT systems should be implemented in parallel as a cost-effective mechanism to provide high-speed service in key

corridors and as a complementary feeder service to the mass transit systems.

- BRT systems should be implemented as a primary service, where expected travel volumes are not very high and in congested corridors with no available road space.
- Public transit systems should be prioritized in urban signaling so that the capacity is well utilized.
- Traffic rules and regulations must be enforced more stringently.
- Private vehicle usage should be streamlined, if not discouraged, by increased ownership costs, driving license costs, parking changes and so on. All such charges levied should be re-invested into future developments and upgrading of existing services.
- Transport infrastructure must be redesigned and rebuilt to make them more pedestrian friendly and conducive for cyclists.
- Land-use and transport planning must be better coordinated through transit-oriented development and also by incorporating stricter environmental and energy efficiency standards.

References

Cohen, B. 2006. "Urbanization in Developing Countries: Current Trends, Future Projections, and Key Challenges for Sustainability." *Technology in Society* 28, nos. 1–2, pp. 63–80.

Pucher, J.Z., R. Peng, N. Mittal, Y. Zhu, and N. Korattyswaroopam. 2007. "Urban Transport Trends and Policies in China and India: Impacts of Rapid Economic Growth." *Transport Reviews* 27, no. 4, pp. 379–410.

Segel, A., and O.O. Hartleben. 2015. "Building Cities: A Technical Note." HBS/9-213-006.

Serafeim, G., and D. Freiberg. 2017. "The Future of Mobility: Economic, Environmental and Social Implications." HBS/9-118-008.

UN Report on World Population Prospects. 2017. Available online at https://esa.un.org/unpd/wpp/Publications/Files/WPP2017_KeyFindings.pdf (accessed on September 30, 2018).

UN-Habitat, Planning and Design for Sustainable Urban Mobility, United Nations Human Settlements Programme Global Report on Human Settlements 2013.

CHAPTER 2

Ahmedabad Bus Rapid Transit System

Background

Sultan Ahmad Shah founded the city of Ahmedabad in 1411 AD, as a walled city on the banks of the Sabarmati River; the commercial capital of the state Gujarat is now the seventh largest in India and the largest city in the state. With a population of six million inhabitants (2001), Ahmedabad covers an area of 466 square kilometers. The city faces many challenges that arise predominantly in maintaining the city's contribution to the state's growth. Ahmedabad represents 25 percent of the urban population of the state and 20 percent of the state's GDP (2001). Its population is forecast to increase to 11 million by 2035. It has registered vehicle strength of 1.4 million and the vehicles' growth rate was about 9 to 10 percent per year. Sustaining the growth from current 440 square kilometers to 1,000 square kilometers in 2035 is possible with the development of a rapid and efficient mass transit system (NIUA 2014).

Transport System Before the Project

Ahmedabad Municipal Corporation (AMC) operates a well-managed public transit system known as the Ahmedabad Municipal Transportation System (AMTS). However, due to the resource crisis and operating system inefficiency, the fleet size has gone down to 450 in 2005. This resulted in a significant reduction in ridership also. While the share of public transit has decreased, the share of private unorganized sector (such as auto-rickshaws) has increased. In the city, about 35,000 auto-rickshaws operated to provide 10 percent of the total urban mobility. In addition, these rickshaws used adulterated fuel, which greatly affects the air quality.

As a result, the city of Ahmedabad was among the top three cities in the list of 88 critically polluted cities in India as in 2004.

In 2005, the average daily passengers riding AMTS was 3.5 lakh. AMC undertook a restructuring exercise in 2006, invited private operators to operate based on gross contracts, which led to the doubling of the fleet size of AMTS. Today, AMTS with a fleet size of about 1,000 vehicles caters to about 0.83 million passengers every day. Moreover, methane is the primary fuel used by most of the buses and rickshaws in the city, which contributes to a significant reduction in the pollution arising out of public transport (NIUA 2014).

Traffic problems in urban areas are increasing due to rapid population growth and increasing number of vehicles that result in excessive delays, travel time and reduced speed on urban roads. Public transport service quality has deteriorated rapidly over the last decade. The impact is visible in terms of increased congestion on the city roads and deterioration of air quality. Reducing these problems requires a sustainable transit system. Promoting bus rapid transit (BRT) is a viable option to improve service delivery in public passenger transport, in particular, as it affects the most widespread form of transportation in Ahmedabad road transport. The key is to relieve congestion, provide better transit choices in terms of rapid and convenient mobility, reduced incidents, and preserve for a sustainable environment with less pollutants. There are additional incurred costs and benefits for different stake-holders such as government, private carriers, regular commuters, unskilled labor and the urban support services.

The Rationale for BRTS

In a developing country like India, urban growth is phenomenal and generally unplanned. Agglomeration is unpredictable and quite often depends on a multitude of factors that are beyond control; most cities grow on their own. The primary impact is on urban mobility. Transportation sector growth and planning do not keep pace with the urban growth, both spatially and temporally. Transportation planning and management is often a continuous activity as challenges related to traffic emerge continuously. Various factors led Ahmedabad urban planners to opt for the bus rapid transit system (BRTS) in the city. They are as follows:

- City was characterized by very randomized development, but with localized trips;
- The urban pull was spreading out to wider areas;
- There was an impending need for decongestion;
- Routing flexibility was becoming a priority;
- There was a good scope for both low density and high density passenger movement;
- There was a possibility to leverage public space and improve accessibility;
- BRTS can be operated according to the city ethos; and
- BRTS was an environment friendly urban mobility choice (NIUA 2014).

The Genesis of Ahmedabad BRTS

The Government of India (GoI) announced the Jawaharlal Nehru National Urban Renewal Mission (JNNURM) for urban development and the AMC submitted its proposal to the GoI for the Ahmedabad BRTS project, the first of its kind in the country. JNNURM was an initiative proposed by the GoI and all states were invited to submit proposals for developing and renovate a city in the state. Substantial funds with literally no hidden costs were allocated to the state based on the proposals. States were subject to stringent agreement clauses on expenditure and project completion. Proposal submitted by AMC was approved by the Ministry of Urban Development (MoUD), and AMC initiated the Ahmedabad BRTS project.

The Government of Gujarat (GoG) declared 2005 as the year of urban development (ShaheriVikasVarsh). As part of the declaration, the Urban Development Department of Gujarat undertook several initiatives to address several urban issues such as traffic management, and to improve urban transport systems.

The Gujarat Infrastructure Development Board (GIDB), AMC and Ahmedabad Urban Development Authority (AUDA) jointly developed a comprehensive plan for urban mobility to meet the requirements of Ahmedabad city and implementation of the BRTS. Centre for Environment Planning and Technology (CEPT University) prepared a detailed project report (DPR) for the implementation of the BRTS project in Ahmedabad. The BRTS project was approved in November 2006 and work on the project began in 2007 (NIUA 2014).

Ahmedabad Profile

History

Ahmedabad is located between 22o55′ and 23o08′ north latitude and 72o30′ and 72o42′ east longitude. Gujarat, including Ahmedabad city is very arid and dry. The city has no significant physical characteristics, except for the monsoon fed river Sabarmati. The river divisions the city into two: the fortified, old city on the east bank and a newer development on the west bank.

Demographic Trends

The largest urban area of Ahmedabad covers an area of about 4,200 square kilometers and includes the following:

1. An area of 190 square kilometers under the jurisdiction of AMC,
2. 150 villages around the city under the jurisdiction of the AUDA,
3. Nine municipalities on the outskirts of the city under the jurisdiction of the Urban Development Authority Ahmedabad (AUDA),
4. Gandhinagar and fractions,
5. Chatral, Bopal and other neighboring towns adjoining AUDA (AMC, AUDA, and CEPT University, City Development Plan Ahmedabad 2006–2012).

The area within the limits of AMC consists of:

1. The center of the traditional city within the walls of the fort with the development of relatively high density, high concentration of commercial activities and narrow streets,
2. The eastern sector, which houses large and small industries and low-income residential areas, and

3. A well-planned western sector with large streets housing prominent institutions and high-income residential areas (AMC, AUDA, and CEPT University, City Development Plan Ahmedabad 2006–2012).

The Figure 2.1 provides the graphic representation of periphery of Greater Ahmedabad.

Population under the AMC limit increased from 2.9 million in 1991 to 3.5 million in 2001 and the population of the AUDA area was recorded as 3.9 million in 1991. Ahmedabad's urban area (AUA) is home to 23.25 percent of the urban population of the state in 1991, or about 25 percent in 2001. Compared to other megalopolises in India, Ahmedabad has a low degree of primacy and the distribution of urban population is fairly uniform in Metropolitan and the suburbs.

AMC area covers 190.84 square kilometers, the AUA area is about 350 square kilometers and the AUDA area is 1,330.08 square kilometers (AMC, AUDA, and CEPT University, City Development Plan Ahmedabad 2006–2012). The spatial distribution of the population in the city until 1981 shows that most of the urbanizing population into the city

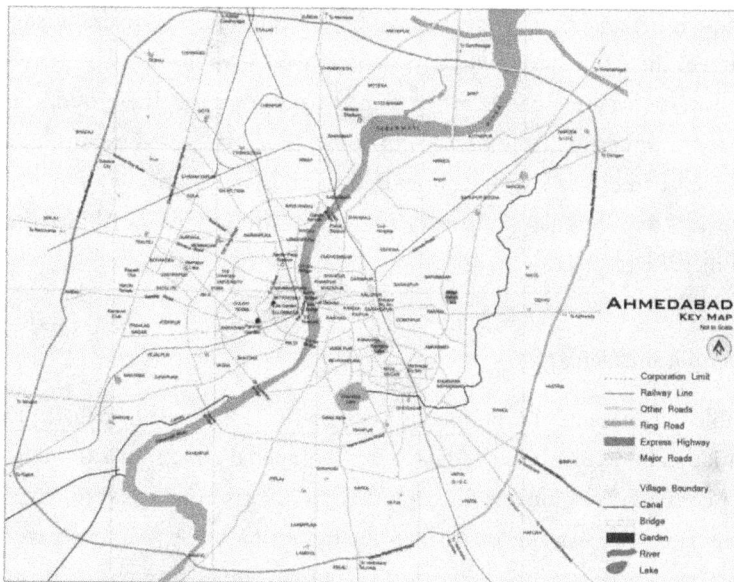

Figure 2.1 **Greater Ahmedabad**

Source: Fact file—a complete Ahmedabad city guide by Dr. Manek Patel.

were concentrated in the former AMC boundaries, particularly in the east. Expansion of peripheral areas began in 1980. Until the 1980s, only the eastern regions, especially the eastern suburbs grew rapidly; later the western suburbs also started expanding rapidly.

Spatial Patterns of Population Change

Table 2.1 compares the decadal population growth of Greater Ahmedabad from 1981 to 2011 with percentage growth for 1991 and 2001.

Ahmedabad region has grown at a moderate pace. Growth rates have fallen annually from 3.2 to 2.2 percent over the past two decades (AMC, AUDA, and CEPT University, City Development Plan Ahmedabad 2006–2012). However, the growth rates have not been consistent and uniform across the city. The population growth within AMC appears to have stabilized (Refer Table 2.1). Areas adjacent to AMC and within AUDA limits showed rapid growth. Similar to global trends, population growth in peripheral areas is more rapid than areas within the city limits. This is partly due to the saturation of urban space occupancy and the consequent development of large-scale housing in peripheral regions. The contradicting spatial occupancy patterns observed in the eastern and western parts of the AMC have replicated to peripheral areas in a similar manner. The western part expands faster than the eastern part. These trends are likely to intensify in the decades to come. Notably, spatial expansion of Ahmedabad city is largely contiguous and relatively compact. Table 2.2 provides with population density decadal growth of Greater Ahmedabad from 1981 to 2001.

Population Density

Table 2.2 presents the population density in Greater Ahmedabad. The variation in density presented indicates that spatial expansion is limited to the contiguous regions around the AMC. The fortified city is very densely populated and has almost reached the saturation levels. Western part of the city under the jurisdiction of AUDA continues to grow, as people prefer to stay in peripheral regions where open spaces are available and possibly better infrastructure can be developed.

Table 2.1 Population growth—greater Ahmedabad

Spatial unit	Population			
	1981	1991	2001	2011
1. Ahmedabad Municipal Corporation (AMC)	2,159,127	2,876,710 (2.9)	3,520,085 (2.0)	5,583,931[1]
1a. Walled City	476,138	398,410 -1.8	372,633 -0.7	367,953 4
1b. East AMC	1,122,073	1,902,868 5.4	2,521,013 2.9	3,908,752[1]
1c. West AMC	463,922	575,433 2.2	675,362 1.6	1,675,179[1]
2. A.U.D.A.	2,721,925	3,756,246 3.3	4709,180 2.3	
2.1a. East AUDA	101,144	128,999 2.5	202,494 4.6	
2.1b. West AUDA	204,923	457,271 8.4	701,424 4.4	
2.1c. AUDA (Rural)	209,826	246,560 1.6	274,391 1.1	
3. Kalol	78,407	92,550 1.7	112,013 1.9	113,153[2]
4. Mehemdabad	22,309	26,103 1.6	30,768 1.7	35,368 3
5. Dehgam	24,868	31,378 2.4	38,082 2.0	42,632[2]
6. Sanand	22,465	25,674 1.3	32,417 2.4	41,530[2]
7. Other areas outside AUDA	264,555	309,871 1.6	334,531 0.8	
8. Gandhinagar	199,353	280,234 3.5	373,663 2.9	
8a. Gandhinagar (GNA)	62,443	123,359 7.0	195,926 4.7	206,167[2]
8b. Rest of Gandhinagar	136,910	156,875 1.4	177,737 1.3	
GREATER AHMEDABAD	3,185,833	4,346,351 3.2	5,417,374 2.2	6,361,084[2]

Source: CEPT/GIDB 2005 Ahmedabad BRTS Report No. 1 (CEPT/GIDB 2005)

Urban Economy

Ahmedabad plays a crucial role in the economic development of Gujarat, as the city hosts a number of a high productivity industries and commercial establishments. Ahmedabad has seven percent of the total population of the state and about 20 percent of the urban population; and it contributed 17 percent of the state's income in 1995. The city of Ahmedabad is home to 21.5 percent of state's factories, which employs 18 percent of workers, as in 2000. In 1981, before the crisis of the textile industries,

Table 2.2 Population density—greater Ahmedabad

Patial unit	Persons/hectare		
	1981	1991	2001
1. Ahmedabad Municipal Corporation (AMC)	113	151	184
1a. Walled City	716	599	560
1b. East AMC	79	134	178
1c. West AMC	109	135	159
2. A.U.D.A.	11	61	77
2a. East AUDA	6	7	11
2b. West AUDA	13	28	43
2c. AUDA (Rural)	12	16	14
3. Kalol	27	31	38
4. Mehemdabad	19	22	26
5. Dehgam	11	13	16
6. Sanand	6	7	9
7. Other areas outside AUDA	8	9	10
8. Gandhinagar	5	7	9
8a. Gandhinagar (GNA)	24	47	75
8b. Rest of Gandhinagar	4	4	5
GREATER AHMEDBAD	12	16	20

Source: CEPT/GIDB 2005 Ahmedabad BRTS Report No.1 (CEPT/GIDB 2005).

the city of Ahmedabad used to represent 19.3 percent of factories and 27.7 percent of state workers (AMC, AUDA, and CEPT University, City Development Plan Ahmedabad 2006–2012).

Ahmedabad city accounts for nearly 19 percent of the state's urban workforce and around 60 percent of the district's workforce. After economic liberalization of the early 1990s, Ahmedabad experienced a significant sectoral change. Chemical and petrochemical industries in the southern districts of Gujarat grew very rapidly. The investment figures show a significant decrease in the share of manufacturing industries in Ahmedabad and its neighborhood. However, services sector including business and commerce, transport and communications, construction and health care appears to be growing. The Workers Participation Rate

(WPR) or percentage of the workforce in Ahmedabad was 32 percent in 2001, compared to 33 percent of the state's urban WPR. Table 2.3 categorizes the sectoral occupation of the workforce in Ahmedabad and its changes over the years.

Table 2.3 provides the comparative analysis of sectorial distribution of occupational pattern of Ahmedabad, with percentage wise distribution of each sector from 1971 to 2001.

Land Use

Spatial disposition and land usage determine the population distribution patterns and the demand for infrastructure in the city. AUDA undertakes the land usage planning of areas under its jurisdiction. As mentioned earlier, the area under AUDA is grouped into several sub-units of secondary administrative jurisdiction. The demarcated area of Ahmedabad urban complex consisting of areas under AMC and the adjacent AMC extension is planned for substantial development in the next ten years.

Land-Use in AUDA Area

The built-up land in the entire AUDA limits is nearly 50 percent of 1,294.65 square kilometers. The waterbodies and wastelands cover 12 percent and 17 percent of the surface area, respectively. Industries account for nine percent of the region (AMC, AUDA, and CEPT University, City Development Plan Ahmedabad 2006–2012). According to the Gujarat state government policy, major industrial development is prohibited within 24 kilometers of the AMC limit within the jurisdiction of AUDA. As per the current policies, the Government allocates specific areas for development of light industries. Figure 2.2 illustrates the AUDA land use map.

Table 2.4 presents the distribution of land use patterns in AUDA Area with percentage wise distribution of land use in AUDA area for the year 1997.

The following map provides with the graphic representation of land use in AUDA area.

Table 2.3 Occupational pattern of Ahmedabad

Sectors		Categories	1971 No.s	1971 %	1991 No.s	1991 %	2001 No.s	2001 %
Primary sector	I	Cultivation	839	0.19	2,659	0.32	1,168	0.10
	II	Agricultural laborers	613	0.14	1,889	0.23	1,133	0.10
	III	Livestock, forestery, fishing, and so on and allied activities	2,749	0.61	5,444	0.65	A	
	IV	Mining and quarrying	2,557	0.57	1,932	0.23		
	Total		6,758	1.50	11,924	1.43		
Secondary sector	V-A	Manufacturing and processing in household industries	6,857	1.52	6,479	0.78	34,624	3.09

						B
	V-B	Manufacturing and processing in other than household industries	204,255	45.39	308,183	37.07	A+B = 1,085,070 (96.71%)
	VI	Construction	14,203	3.16	38,197	4.59	
	Total		225,315	50.08	352,859	42.44	
Tertiary sector	VII	Trade and commerce	88,239	19.61	212,051	25.50	
	VIII	Transport. Storage and communication	32,779	7.28	75,446	9.07	
	IX	Other services (Other than those aforementioned, for example, politics, social work, Govt. services, teaching, entertainment, and so on	96,864	21.53	179,179	21.55	
	Total		217,882	48.42	466,676	56.13	
Grand total			449,955	100.00	831,459	100.00	831,459	100.00

Source: (AMC, AUDA, and CEPT University, City Development Plan Ahmedabad 2006–2012).

Source: (AMC, AUDA and CEPT University, City Development Plan Ahmedabad 2006–2012).

Land Use in AMC Area

As per the land usage survey taken in 1997, more than one third (36 percent) of the total area is allocated for residential purposes, followed by 15 percent of the area for industries. Large packets of land (24 percent) are typically vacant, especially in newly acquired areas of AMC. Only 9.5 percent of the total area is under the high power transmission networks against the standard allocated 15 to 18 percent as specified by the UDPFI standard norms (AMC, AUDA, and CEPT University, City Development Plan Ahmedabad 2006–2012). This implies less urban space is exposed to power supply network related risks. Figure 2.2 illustrates the distribution of existing land space as per urban planning of 1997. Figure 2.3 illustrates the distribution of land space as planned in the urban development plan of 2011. Tables 2.4 and 2.5 represent the proposed and existing land use planning of area under AMC and area excluding AMC respectively.

Table 2.5 provides distribution of existing land use patterns in AMC area for the year 1997 by indicating the percentage wise distribution of all AMC land area. Figure 2.3 illustrates the land usage of AMC in 1997.

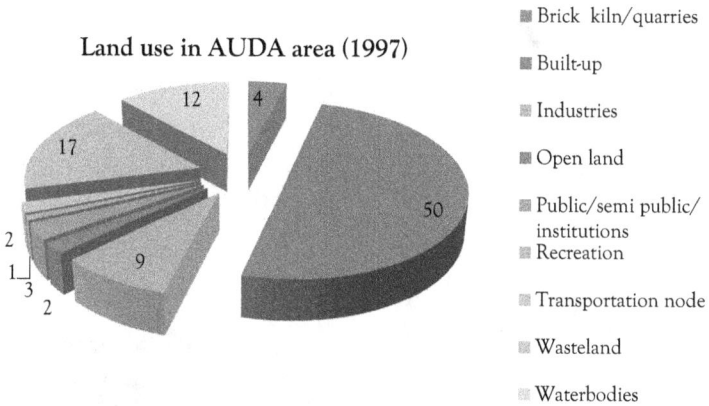

Figure 2.2 AUDA land use map
Source: City development plan Ahmedabad (CDP 2006–2012).

Table 2.4 Land use in AUDA area (1997)

Sr. No.	Spatial unit	Percentage (%)
1	Brick kiln/quarries	4
2	Built-up	50
3	Industries	9
4	Open land	2
5	Public/semi public/institutions	3
6	Recreation	1
7	Transportation node	2
8	Wasteland	17
9	Waterbodies	12

Table 2.5 Existing land use of AMC area (1997)

Sr. No.	AMC land area distribution	Percentage (%)
1	AMC plots	2
2	Commercial	2
3	Educational	2
4	Hospitals	1
5	Industrial	15
6	Open/vacant land	24
7	Railway land	2
8	Residential	36
9	Road	7
10	Village site/Gamtal	5
11	Waterbodies	4

Existing land use of AMC area (1997)

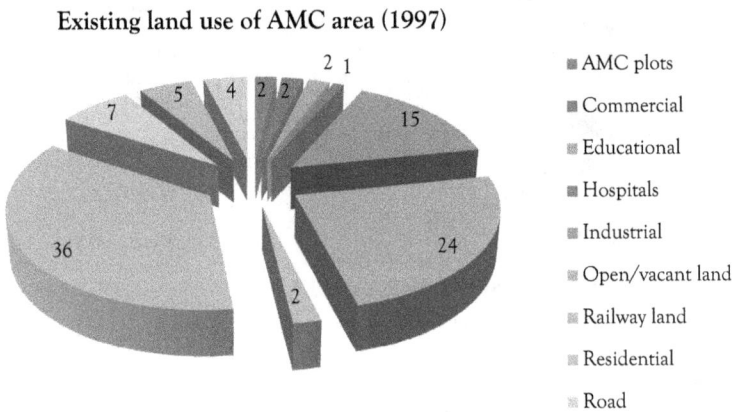

Figure 2.3 Land usage of AMC in 1997

Source: City development plan Ahmedabad (CDP 2006–2012).

Table 2.6 provides with the distribution of proposed land use patterns in AMC area for the year 2011 by indicating the percentage wise distribution proposed land use of AMC area. Figure 2.4 illustrates the proposed land use of AMC in 2011.

The Table 2.7 compares the existing and proposed land use patterns in AMC Area between 1997 and 2011 as percentage wise distribution of land use area.

Table 2.6 *Proposed land use of AMC area (2011)*

Sr. No.	Spatial units	Percentage (%)
1	Agri./openspace	9
2	Commercial	1
3	Education	2
4	General industrial	11
5	Residential	44
6	Roads and railways	11
7	Special development area	10
8	Special industrial	4
9	Walled city and Gamtal	3
10	Waterbodies (including rivers)	5

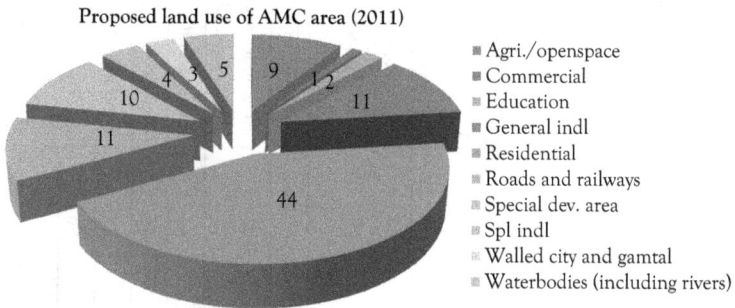

Proposed land use of AMC area (2011)

■ Agri./openspace
■ Commercial
▥ Education
■ General indl
■ Residential
▥ Roads and railways
▥ Special dev. area
▣ Spl indl
▨ Walled city and gamtal
▨ Waterbodies (including rivers)

Figure 2.4 *Proposed land use of AMC in 2011*

Source: City development plan Ahmedabad (CDP 2006–2012).

The Table 2.8 compares existing and proposed land use patterns in AUC area (excluding AMC area) between 1997 and 2011 as percentage wise distribution of land use area.

Traffic Generating Activities

The nature and location of regions of economic activities, as against residential areas determine the demand for travel around a city. Ahmedabad majorly contributes to the economic growth and development of the

Table 2.7 *Existing and proposed land use of AMC area*

Sr. No.	Existing land use for AMC area (1997)			Proposed land use for AMC (2011)		
	Use/designation	Total area (Ha.)	% of total area	Use/designation	Total area (Ha.)	% of total area
1	Residential	6,664.44	34.92	Residential	8,340.22	43.70
2	Commercial	472.64	2.47	Walled city and village sites (Gamtal)	645.56	3.38
3	Industrial	2,932.78	15.37	General industrial	2,006.51	10.51
4	Open/vacant land	4,473.36	23.44	Special industrial	786.72	4.12
5	Village site/Gamtal	895.59	4.69	Commercial	263.06	1.38
6	Education	344.19	1.80	Agricultural/recreational/open Space/gardens	1,643.60	8.61
7	AMC plots	467.18	2.45	Education	387.30	2.03
8	Hospitals	98.36	0.52	Area under reservations now designated as special development area	1,955.37	10.25
9	Burial ground/grave yard	86.54	0.45	Road and railways	2,117.67	11.10
10	Water bodies	850.55	4.46	Water bodies (including rivers)	937.97	4.92
11	Roads	1,426.65	7.47	Total area	19,084	100.00
12	Railway land	372.00	1.96			
	Total	19,084.00	100.00			

Source: Revised draft development plan of AUDA—2011 part I, vol 2.

Table 2.8 *Existing and proposed land use of AUC area (excluding AMC)*

Existing land use of AUC area (excluding AMC area) (1997)				Proposed land use of AUC area (excluding AMC limit): (2011)			
Sr. No.	Land use	Total	% of developed area	Sr. No.	Particulars	Area in hect.	% age of developed land
1	Residential include Gamtal	3,559	38.99	1	Residential, roads, public and semi public		
2	Public and semi public	572	6.27		Type 1 (old residential area)	9,938	34.523
3	Commercial	276	3.02		Type 2 (new residential area)	4,624.24	16.066
4	Industrial	647	7.09	2	Commercial	1,071.92	3.724
5	Railway/roads/airport	406	4.45	3	Industrial	387.58	3.431
6	Water way and tank	3,625	39.72	4	Public activity area	552	1.918
7	Garden open space and P.G	41	0.46	5	Public and semi-public	243	0.844

(Continued)

Table 2.8 (Continued)

| | Existing land use of AUC area (excluding AMC area) (1997) | | | | Proposed land use of AUC area (excluding AMC limit): (2011) | | | |
Sr. No.	Land use	Total	% of developed area	Sr. No.	Particulars	Area in hect.	% age of developed land
	Total	9,126	100	6	Recreational	6,300	21.885
				7	Treatment plants (AUDA, AMC)	745.16	2.589
				8	High flood hazards	524	1.82
				9	Agriculture	3800.42	13.202
					Total area	28,787	100

Source: Revised draft development plan of AUDA—2011 part I, vol. 2.

Residential areas   Commercial areas

Areas under public facilities   Areas under industrial use

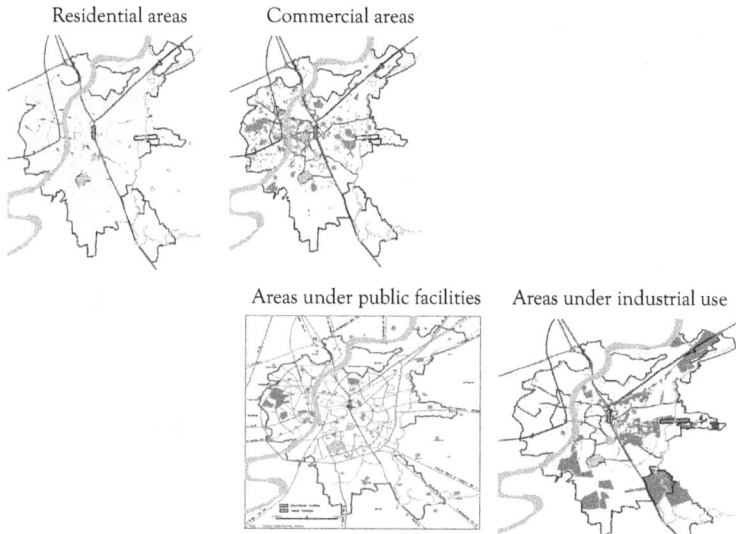

Figure 2.5 Various socio-economic activities in Ahmedabad

Source: Derived from city development strategies, Ahmedabad (2003).

state. Ahmedabad is traditionally considered as a strong industrial base of conventional manufacturing, especially textiles, plastics, machinery and metals and alloys. The city of Ahmedabad represents 21.5 percent of state's factories, which employs 18 percent of workers as of 2000. Until early 1980s, Ahmedabad has a significant presence in textile industry. Known as a center of trade and commerce in western India, Ahmedabad is gradually shifting toward service economy establishments from the more conservative manufacturing industries. Tertiary sectors such as trading, small businesses, and commercial establishments are becoming more prominent. Figure 2.5 illustrates the concentration of various socio-economic activities in Ahmedabad.

Summary

The AUDA caters to a population of 45 lakhs (as of 2001), of which 78 percent is in the municipality. Ahmedabad is the largest city in terms of population size and contribution to state's income. Over the years, rapid urbanization has forced people to move to peripheral regions of the city. Severe shortages in urban space led to increased number of development of high-rise structures, exerting further stress on the inadequate infrastructure. Over the next 10 years, the population is expected to increase from 35 to 46 lakh in AMC and 46 to 60 lakh in Ahmedabad urban complex; challenges in planning urban growth are too many and grave.

However the city growth has been radial, compact and contained, while some industrial activities have moved to the suburbs. Exploration of development-oriented transit as a mechanism for urban planning would be an essential tool. As can be observed, land-use planning efforts were successful enough in Ahmedabad to contain the pace of vicious expansions. Given that the city is prone to earthquakes and torrential floods, disaster prevention planning should be essentially integrated with every urban planning activity.

Existing Transportation System—Vehicles, Facilities and Performance

System Components

Transport in Ahmedabad city is facilitated by a well-laid out road urban network, state and national highways, railway lines, domestic and international airway services. The city and state demography is characterized by enterprising, business minded and networked society with aspirations for commercial growth and international mobility. Vehicle growth has been rapid, as possession of vehicles is both a need and a symbol of pride. Existing transport infrastructure is therefore, heavily congested and consequently air pollution due to transport emissions is on the rise.

Vehicles

The state of Gujarat was formed in 1961 and there were only 43,000 registered vehicles, then. This figure increased to more than 70 lakh vehicles in 2004, an increase of 160 times in four decades. In the recent past, number of vehicles has been rising very high. In the years 2001 to 2002, the increase in the number of registered vehicles was 0.43 million. This increased to 0.51 million and 0.57 million in 2002 to 2003 and 2003 to 2004, respectively. Ahmedabad district has 1.49 million registered vehicles in 2004. Of these, 73 percent are two wheelers. As a district,

Ahmedabad has 11 percent of the state's population and accounts for about 21 percent of state's registered vehicles (CDP 2006–2012). This high density and rapid growth of vehicles have aggravated the transport related challenges in Ahmedabad significantly.

The Table 2.9 presents the different types of vehicles in Ahmedabad as a percentage distribution. Figure 2.6 illustrates the distribution of different vehicle types in Ahmedabad.

Table 2.9 Composition of vehicles in Ahmedabad

Sr. No.	Type of vehicles	Percentage (%)
1	Bus	1.64
2	Cars	12.5
3	LCV	1.06
4	MUV	4.45
5	Taxi	0.41
6	Trucks	2.03
7	2 Wheelers	72.91
8	3 Wheelers	5.01

Types of vehicles in Ahmedabad

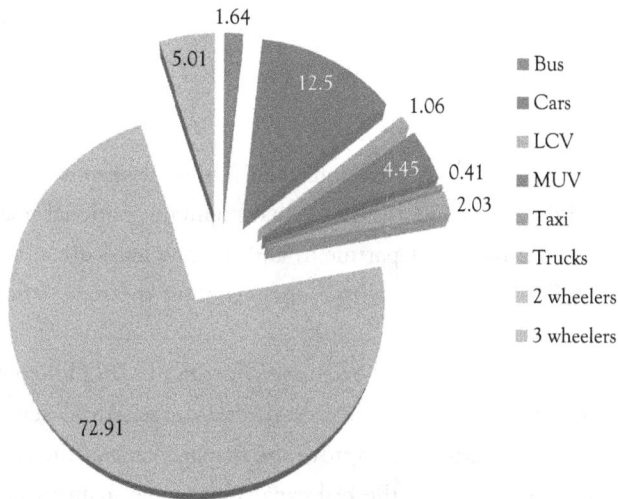

Figure 2.6 Vehicular distributions in Ahmedabad

Source: MoRTH, Gujarat.

Table 2.10 presents the 10-year growth rate of vehicles in Ahmedabad with the comparative data of growth at the national and state levels. Annual increase in the number of vehicles is quite high at a rate of 13 percent, indicating the increasing demand on existing infrastructure.

This table presents the composition of the total number of vehicles in circulation with comparative decadal growth of India, Gujarat and Ahmedabad.

The growth rate of the Gujarat population of vehicles is even higher than the national growth rate because the state economy has consistently performed better than many other states in recent decades. As shown in Table 2.10, the growth pattern of the various vehicle types in Ahmedabad over the last 30 years has been very steep. Two wheelers, three wheelers and transit vehicles (privately operated as unorganized sector) have a significant influence on urban air quality. Ahmedabad has one of the highest growth rates in two-wheeler and three-wheeler motor vehicles. It has experienced 18 times the population growth of vehicles over the past 40 years (1971–2001) with nearly 39 times the population growth in two-wheeler motor vehicles.

Table 2.11 presents the total decadal growth rate of vehicular fleet including (two wheelers, three wheelers and AMTS bus), with percentage increase from 1971 to 2001.

Services

Road Networks

Ahmedabad's land area is more than 3,478 kilometers. National Highway Authority of India (NHAI) that maintains national roads and state roads and buildings department, and the two local urban bodies (AMC and AUDA) develop, manage and maintain the road infrastructure of Ahmedabad.

The AMC operates an extensive network of 1,272 kilometer of roads, 93 percent of which are surface roads (source: AMC statistics outline 2000–2001). Efforts to improve the management of the city's road network have resulted in the real expansion of the main roads of the city. The ratio between the areas under the road is only 7.5 percent of the total area of the city compared to the desired value of 15 to 18 percent.

Table 2.10 *Total number of vehicles in circulation and 10-year growth in India, Gujarat and Ahmedabad*

Year	India		Gujarat		Ahmedabad	
	Total	Decadal growth	Total	Decadal growth	Total	Decadal growth
1961	665,000		43,230		N.A	
1971	1,865,000	180%	147,967	242%	62,922	
1981	5,391,000	189%	522,451	253%	165,620	163%
1991	21,474,000	298%	2,052,391	292%	538,182	225%
2001	54,991,000	156%	5,576,040	172%	1,210,278	125%

Source: MoRTH, Gujarat.

Table 2.11 Total growth of AMTS buses and two or three wheelers, Ahmedabad (1971–2001)

Year	All vehicles		Two wheelers		Three wheelers		AMTS buses	
	Total	Growth	Total	Growth	Total	Growth	Total	Growth
1971	62,922	-	21,702	-	4,865	-	525	-
1981	165,620	163%	86,550	299%	16,741	244%	610	16%
1991	538,182	225%	361,372	318%	38,359	249%	756	24%
2001	1,210,278	125%	863,003	139%	65,868	72%	886	17%
Total growth (71—2001)	1,823%		3,877%		1,253%		69%	

Source: Transport Department, Gujarat, Ahmedabad 2004.

This translates into an average road width of 12 meters. Road density is 6.66 per square kilometer area. The road network in the central area (the walled city of AMC) is narrow and overgrown with vegetation, unorganized parking and informal business activities (CDP 2006–2012).

Accidents

In Ahmedabad, according to recent reports more than 2,600 traffic accidents occurred in 2001. Approximately 160 to 200 people lost lives in these accidents. Table 2.12 presents the decadal population in millions with vehicles, accidents (including fatal and accidents per thousand vehicles) and fatality rate from 1961 to 2001.

Effects on Air Quality

There was a rapid increase in the ownership of motorcycles in Ahmedabad between 1971 and 2001, which also led to increased pollution levels. Vehicular pollution alone accounts for 60 to 70 percent of the total pollution in the (CDP 2006–2012). The major cause of air pollution in Ahmedabad is due to two-wheeler vehicles and auto-rickshaws. Trends in pollution levels in Ahmedabad are shown in Figure 2.7.

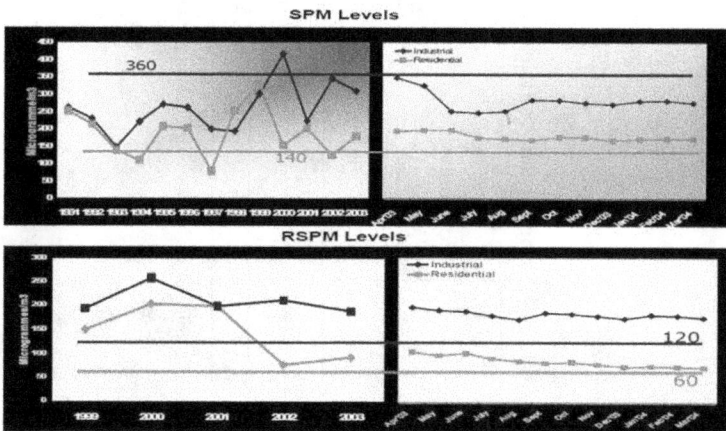

Figure 2.7 Pollution levels in Ahmedabad

Source: Gujarat Pollution Control Board.

Table 2.12 Population, vehicles and accidents in the city of Ahmedabad

Year	Population (Million)	Vehicles	Accidents	Fatal accidents	Accident rate (per 10,000 vehicles)	Fatality rate
1961	1.26	N.A.	643	38	N.A.	5.91
1971	1.76	45,268	866	73	191.31	8.43
1981	2.38	120,514	1,676	144	139.07	8.59
1991	2.95	431,783	2,931	192	67.88	6.55
2001	3.7	1,005,870	2,716	162	27.02	5.96

Source: Safe traffic advocacy cell, school of planning, CEPT University.

The RSPM and SPM levels allowed in accordance with National Ambient Air Quality Standards (NAAQS) were consistently higher in industrial and residential areas.

Public Transit

Overview

In the city of Ahmedabad, public transit is operated, managed and maintained by AMTS. It is a municipal agency service that operates about 550 buses, of which only about 350 are on the road every day. Over the years, the AMTS has experienced a rapid decline in its ridership numbers due to increasing numbers of two-wheelers, escalating property prices, wide real-estate development, lack of road rationalization and poor transport infrastructure to meet the public transit demand. Until around 2006, AMTS has significantly improved their services (routes and fleet) and the ridership per day had increased to 0.65 million (CDP 2006–2012).

Operations and Details

AMTS operates around 0.25 million trips every day. It operates about 150 lines with a bus fleet size of 540; use of fleet was still low. The average route length is about 17 kilometer and lengths of route range from 5 kilometer to 57 kilometer; approximately 55 percent of buses run on long roads of 10 to 20 kilometer, with 30 to 90 minutes of trip time. Halt points were located at an average distance of about 410 meters, which is favored for end-mile connectivity for commuters; however frequent halts result in more delays and more travel time. Moreover, the average speed of AMTS is limited to about 20 kilometer per hour with the philosophy that less speed would be safer. Initial planning of the role of AMTS was to provide bus services exclusively within the municipality; gradually AMTS extended its services to areas on the outer periphery of the city with increasing dependence of the urban and remote areas on each other. As a result, the operational coverage of AMTS increased to 375 square kilometers compared to the previous 198 square kilometers of the city (AMC, AUDA, and CEPT University, City Development Plan Ahmedabad 2006–2012).

Table 2.13 AMTS-2008 status

Sr. No.	Details	Particulars
(a)	Routes	154 full routes and with addition of shuttles, routes are 187
(b)	Road length under transit routes	573 kilometers
(c)	No. of bus stops	1398
(d)	No. of terminals	6
(e)	No. of depot/workshop	1 (private operators have own facility)
(f)	Fleet size	1,022
(g)	Fleet utilization	85%
(h)	Vehicle utilization per day	210 kilometers
(i)	Average speeds	18.6
(j)	Occupancy ratio	65%
(k)	Passenger per day: 2006–2007	746,294 (Feb 2008: 936,886)
(l)	Daily revenue (2006–2007)	Rs. 2,587,416
(m)	Daily expenditure	Rs. 44,792,521

Source: AUDA and Gov. of Gujarat.

Table 2.13 presents the detailed operational status of AMTS for the year 2008.

Fares and Occupancy Levels

Based on periodic rise in fuel prices, AMTS has consistently increased the average effective fare rates. However, these increases could not still break-even the operational expenses of AMTS. There has also been a steady decline in the occupancy ratio from about 71 percent in 1991–1992 to about 54 percent in 2004–2005 (CDP 2006–2012). This is indicative of the fact that AMTS has considerably lost the patronage of their services and the increasing availability of personal mobility choices.

Financial Performance

Similar to other urban transit services in the nation, operating losses experienced by AMTS was irrevocable. Majorly, this is attributed to the lack of political will to increase fares appropriately, to target specific commuter groups and offer them attractive travel choices with fair prices, lack of proper control and regulation of free rides by fringe groups, and enforcement of rules. The net result is the loss of productivity of the service provider and sub-optimal mobility choice for the commuters.

Update—CNG Routes

Later, the state government approved 126 routes that could be operated on natural gas/LPG as fuel to meet Bharat-II standards. This required operators to transform their buses along these routes on per kilometer basis. The lease is for five years with an option for two more years. Under the contract, the minimum distance traveled by operating bus in one day is 233 kilometer (CDP 2006–2012). AMC reserves advertising rights with them (as a means of generating income).

The Design of BRTS

Introduction

The proposed BRTS was a high quality, ultra-modern, commuter-oriented rapid transit system to ensure fast, comfortable, economical and environmental friendly mobility choice to urban citizen. With the introduction of the BRTS, the total flow of traffic was expected to increase, as the BRT system was a planned, dedicated transit with private participation; which was a radical shift in Indian urban transit systems. The development of Phase I BRTS of 58.3 kilometer consists of six sections of roads of different lengths and right of way (RoW) with routes dedicated for BRT (AMC, AUDA, and CEPT University 2006–2012). In addition, in the corridors of BRT services, AMTS services would act as primary feed service providers. After the development of Phases 1 and 2, they were planned to be integrated. Based on the detailed assessment, a 30 kilometer network was identified in Phase 2, and a total of 88 kilometer in both the phases (AMC, CEPT, Lea, and ITDP 2008).

Identification and Selection of Corridors

Identification of corridors was a major task in planning, implementing and operating of BRTS. Given that, the available resource of public transport systems is poor, both in quality and in quantity and there is not a single transit dealer to offer high-frequency public transport services, against an increasing demand, the city experienced congestion too often. In light of this, the objective of developing BRTS as a strategic intervention was to provide a better transit choice as well as to improve public perception of public services by leveraging the latent demand for transit, and to improve air quality and regulate urban agglomeration.

Framework

The guiding principles for the selection of corridors are, that:

1. Could accommodate BRTS treatments,
2. Could be implemented quickly and economically,
3. Could contribute to alleviating transport problems considerably,
4. Can improve mobility opportunities for a large segment of the population,
5. Provide opportunities for improved land usage,
6. Provide enough potential for cost recovery,
7. Fair possibility to integrate with other existing modes of public transport, as well as any future expansion plans (AMC, AUDA, and CEPT University 2006–2012).

The selection of corridors was carried out in three steps with the aforementioned principles.

Step 1: Identification of potential BRTS corridors
To identify potential corridors, a thorough monitoring of the road networks was essential.

Step 2: Assessment of corridors with regards to

1. Demand (current and potential)
2. Technical feasibility for the implementation of BRTS treatment
3. Overall system wide impacts

The potential demand for inbound transit travel is based on BRT intra-travel corridor and transit trade. The technical feasibility of implementing

BRTS treatment includes assessment of road width, length of corridor, number and nature of bottlenecks, and environmental and social issues. Based on demand and feasibility, corridors were ranked for performance on a scale of 1 to 5.

Step 3: Priorities for exclusive BRT systems and for mixed operations based on:

1. Implementation considerations
2. Operational considerations
3. Integration issues (AMC, AUDA, and CEPT University 2006–2012)

BRT was planned to be developed as 88 kilometer of fast transit corridors in two phases. The corridors selected as part of Phase 1 were mainly the rings in Ahmedabad. In the design of Phase 1, current and potential demands were the main considerations for the selection of corridors. Since the concept was implemented for the first time, often RoW availability and ease of implementation dominated the decision choices. Corridors where implementation was more difficult, but had a higher demand were included in the later stages. Limiting the overall size of the project was also a factor to remove some of the critical links from Phase 1. Figure 2.8 illustrates the phasing plan of Ahmedabad BRTS corridor.

Services and Routes

The operational plan is the backbone of any public transport. The main components of the operational plan are as follows:

1. Definition of the path
2. Optimal usage of the fleet
3. Frequency during rush and peak hours
4. Station wise timing of each route
5. Identification of transfer points to provide adequate infrastructure
6. Evaluate the boarding/alighting demand at each bus station for sizing
7. Location and size of the terminal

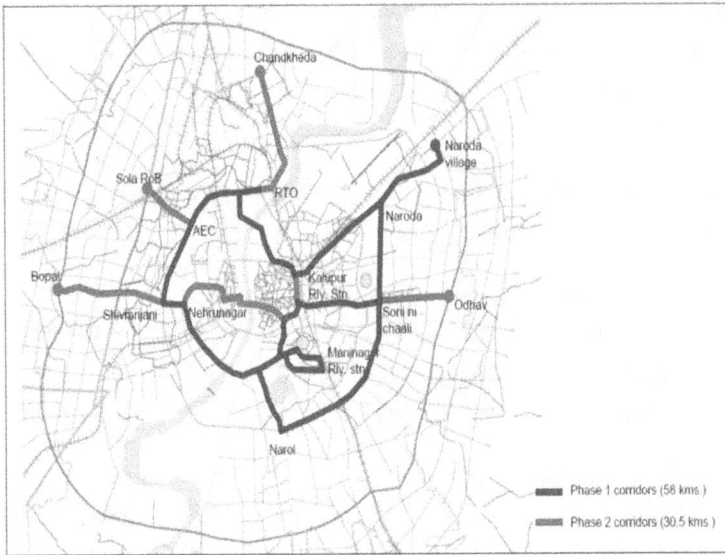

Figure 2.8 **BRTS *phasing of corridors***

Source: AUDA and Gov. of Gujarat.

The operational plan not only provides the road structure for BRT operations but also the routing plan for streamlined AMTS operations. This is necessary for the two systems to complement each other, rather than to compete. Estimating transit demand would lead to estimating the evolution of demand for existing users under different operating conditions, estimating changes in public transport services, assessing changes in the mode of transit and intermediate halt locations and custom traffic generation due to improvements in transit quality. With regard to the three types of itinerary, the transit services operate

1. BRT trunk routes
2. Complementary routes (AMTS)
3. BRT feeder routes

Based on an evaluation of existing routes and travel needs, a set of services was chosen for better transit provisioning, that is, 10 BRT trunk routes, 21 BRT feeders and 60 complementary services (AMC, CEPT,

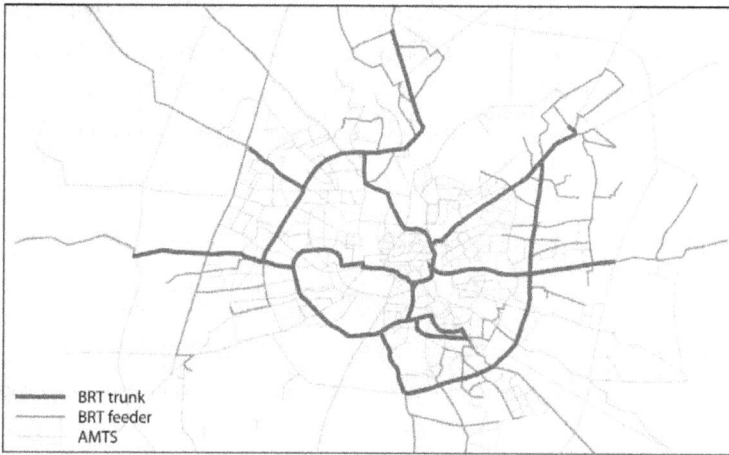

Figure 2.9 Operational plan for Phases 1 and 2

Source: AUDA and Gov. of Gujarat.

Lea, and ITDP 2008). Figure 2.9 illustrates the entire transport network of Ahmedabad with BRT trunk, BRT feeder and the AMTS services.

Policy Issues

Median Lanes

The proposed plan states that the bus lanes were mostly separated by the physical separation volume of the current traffic. The strategical placement of these bus lanes can be in the center of the roadside (median bus lanes) or on the side (side lanes reserved for buses). For the city of Ahmedabad, given the limits of the width of the road, invasions, the threat of livestock and traffic disruption, the recommended choice was to have median lane option of BRT tracks.

Closed System

In a closed system, BRTS is limited to BRT buses. BRT operators are the only beneficiaries who are responsible and accountable for efficiency and maintenance. The recommended choice in Ahmedabad was to have closed corridors through which it was intended to develop an exclusive

BRT system lane. The physical separation between BRT busway from the rest of the traffic by a physical barrier was absolutely necessary. However, given the criticality of the services, the firefighters and ambulances should be allowed to enter and use the BRT lane in emergency situations (AMC, AUDA, and CEPT University 2006–2012).

Exclusive Corridor

The presence of another service such as AMTS in the mixed traffic lanes would not only weaken the ridership but also profitability of the new system as well. An exclusive corridor was expected to create congestion and reduce available space of lanes for traffic. Therefore, the rapid transit corridors that have BRT lanes should have only BRT bus system operational. Other services were not allowed to operate in dedicated BRT lanes. However, the BRT buses will share other AMTS minor routes, where there is no provision for bus lanes; which is a mixed corridor.

Bus Technology

The types of vehicles proposed for the BRT system had variable capacity as shown in the following table.

Table 2.14 presents the details of different vehicle capacity including type, number of passenger and length of vehicle.

However, to begin with, the recommended option was the use of standard buses to accommodate 60 to 70 passengers at a time (CEPT 2006). Buses operating in the BRTS could be made anywhere in India

Table 2.14 Vehicle capacity

Sr. No.	Vehicle type	Typical number of passenger	Typical vehicle length (m)
1	Vans	10–16	3
2	Mini buses	25–35	6
3	Standard buses (low floor)	60–80	12
4	Articulated buses	120–170	18
5	Bi-articulated buss	240–270	24

and then assembled in Ahmedabad. Bus technology to reduce emissions was considered essential. In this context, it was also important to study the possibility of deploying the standard buses with the necessary height adjustment of floor, seats, and so on, and to be operated with compressed natural gas (CNG).

Advanced Technology

The use of intelligent transport systems (ITS) to improve customer comfort, speed, reliability and safety are to be considered in future. Applications that can be developed using Information and Communication Technology (ICT) included operational control, ticketing systems, information system and traffic control system.

Control of Operations

A key element of BRT operations was the ability to monitor and control the bus fleet. Thus, the bus schedules can be adhered to and thereby to provide a reliable service to commuters. Passenger services can be improved by providing real-time information on bus operations. The proposal was to use automatic vehicle location system (AVLS) to track the movement of buses in real-time. Important features such as the position of each bus, monitoring and control of buses using communication systems, information system for passengers in bus stops were under the purview of AVLS.

Bus Location and Control

Moreover for real-time communication to commuters as well as pricing purposes, certain other measurements are necessary. Tracking the bus location, based on distance travelled and the transit time with accurate data is pertinent since the number of kilometers run as per the schedule provided by the Janmarg Operations Department is the basis for all the payments.

On the dashboard of the bus, few devices are installed to operate as an integrated module for

1. Location tracking using global positioning system (GPS)
2. General packet radio service (GPRS) for transmitting location data to the central control center
3. GSM (Global Mobile Communications System) or Code Division Multiple Access (CDMA) for emergency voice communication (AMC, CEPT, Lea, and ITDP 2008).

The system architecture includes the use of Virtual Private Network (VPN), a network of wireless communication service providers to collect data by the service provider's server in the central control center server. The security protocol of Ahmedabad BRTS is designed in 128-bit encryption to protect data during transmission. Janmarg operates the control center, and monitors real-time bus movements.

Passenger Information System

The passenger information system includes three components

1. Inside the bus: The next station's arrival information is communicated in audio-visual format apart from the on-board ad systems that have their own database of routes and stops. Based on the route on which the bus runs, commuters receive information about the position of the bus, the next stop and route related information from the GPS module.
2. In stations: The following bus line and estimated time of arrival are communicated at bus stations. Stations and terminals have screens with a decoder module that decodes only received information about the routes that are likely to reach next at that position and the estimated time of arrival.
3. Outside the bus: Bus line and destination stop information are displayed outside the bus.

Design Considerations

Geometric Design

Appropriate geometric design standards for road design in Phase 1 were proposed. The development of these standards was by taking into account the wide streets with 30 meters RoW and more. However, in Phase 2, the available line varied from 18 meters to 60 meters. Therefore, BRTS proposed changes to the rules; geometric design standards established for the project are as follows:

Table 2.15 presents the geometric design standards of roads for BRTS project Phase I and Phase II.

Table 2.15 Geometric design standards

No.	Description	Design standards (min–max)
1	Right of way	
i)	ROW	18, 24, 35–60 meters
2	Design speed	
	RoW in M	Kilometer per hour
i)	60 meters	80
ii)	40–60 meters	60
iii)	18, 24, 35–40 meters	40
3	Geometric design	
4	Cross sectional elements	
I	Lane widths	
A	Bus lanes	3.5 + 3.5 meters
B	Carriage	9 to 11.25 meters
C	Parking	2.0 + 3.5 meters
D	Service road	3.5 to 7 meters
E	Cycle track	2.0 meters
f	Pedestrian pathway	2 to 3.5 meters
II	Cross slope	2%
a	Median bus lanes	2%
b	Carriageway	2%
c	Parking	2%
d	Service lane	2%
e	Cycle track	2%
f	Pedestrian pathway	2%
5	Shyness strip at the median side	0.25 meter
6	Safe sight stopping distance	60–120 meters
7	Minimum radius of curvature for horizontal alignment	

(Continued)

Table 2.15 (Continued)

No.	Description	Design standards (min–max)
I	Requiring no super elevator	1,400 meters
II	Desirable requiring 4% super elevation	265 meters
III	Absolute minimum requiring 2.5% super elevation	230 meters
8	Vertical alignment	
I	Minimum distance between PVI	150 meters
II	Minimum length of vertical curve	50 meters
III	K value-for-Sag curve	30 meters
IV	K value-for-Crest curve	35 meters
9	Gradient	
I	Maximum	4%
II	Desirable	2%
III	Minimum	0.50%
IV	In kerbed sections	
V	Desirables minimum	0.5%
Vi	Absolute minimum	0.3%
Vii	Desirables maximum for pedestrians ramps	10%
Viii	Desirable maximum for cycle tracks	3%
10	Maximum grade change not requiring a vertical curve	0.6%
11	Minimum vertical clearance to road bridge over road	5.5 meters
12	Minimum vertical clearance to road bridge over rail	6.75 meters
13	Super elevation	
I	Maximum	4%
II	Minimum	2.50%
14	Rate of change of super elevation	1 in 150
15	Bus median	
I	Between bus lane and mixed traffic	0.5 to 1 meter
Ii	Transition slope in median	1 in 15
16	Intersections	
I	Length of storage lane (including 50 meters taper) for right turning	130 meters
Ii	Minimum length of acceleration lane (including 80 meters taper)	180 meters

Iii	Minimum length of deceleration lane (including 80 meters taper)	120 meters
Iv	Maximum radius for left turn	30 meters
V	Maximum radius for right turn	15 meters
Vi	Width of turning lane (inner radius of 30 meters)	5.5 meters
Vii	Rate of taper (minimum)	1 in 15
Viii	Minimum size of channelizing island	4.5 square meters
Ix	Offset of island from vehicle path	0.3 to 0.6 meter
X	Desirable angle of intersection arm	60–90º
Drainage design		
17	Drain	
I	Minimum longitudinal gradient	0.30%
Ii	Minimum width of drain	0.25 meter
Iii	Minimum diameter of drain	0.45 meter
18	Manholes	
I	Spacing	10–20 meters
Ii	Minimum inside dimension	120 centimeter × 90 centimeter
Iii	Minimum allowable width (in case of shallow manholes up to 1.40 meter)	75 centimeter
Iv	Opening for entry	50 meters clear
Safety measures		
19	Traffic signals	IRC: 93—1985 and better experiences
20	Pedestrian crossings and pathways	IRC: 103—1988 and better experiences
Road furniture		
21	Road signage	IRC: 67—1977 and better experiences
22	Pavement markings	IRC: 35—1977 and better experiences
23	Delineators	IRC: 79—1977 and better experiences
Utilities		
24	Maximum depth of laying for utility lines	
I	Trunk sewer line	2–6 meters
Ii	Water supply line	
a	Service line	0.6–1 meter
b	Trunk line	1–1.5 meter
Iii	Electric cable	

(Continued)

Table 2.15 (Continued)

No.	Description	Design standards (min–max)
a	LT cable	0.6–1 meter
B	HT cable	1.5–2 meters
Iv	Telecommunication cable	
a	Directly laid	0.6–1 meter
b	Laid in ducts	2–3 meters
V	Gas mains and lines	2–3 meters
25	Minimum cover over the top of service line	0.65 meter
26	Clearance for utility lines—horizontal (minimum)	
I	Poles erected for various purpose of street lighting, electric power, tele-communication lines in urban area	
A	For roads with raised kerbs	
	• Minimum (from the edge of raised kerb)	300 millimeter
	• Desirable (from the edge of raised kerb)	600 millimeter
B	For roads without raised kerbs, mini-mum (from the edge of carriageway)	1.5
27	Clearance for overhead utility lines—vertical (minimum)	
I	For ordinary wires and lines carrying very low voltage up-to and including 110 volts for example, telecommuni-cation lines	5.5 meters
Ii	For electric power lines carrying voltage upto and including 650 volts	6.0 meters
Iii	For electric power lines carrying voltage exceeding 650 volts	6.5 meters

Source: (AMC, CEPT, Lea, and ITDP 2008).

Bus Shelter Position

Provision for bus shelter position was before intersections in the transit direction and for effective usage of idle time whenever possible. The average distance between two stops was about 800 kilometers and 55 bus stops were identified through the BRTS network of Phase 1. In the first design, stops designed on the left side in the direction of travel indicated that the doors of the buses would also be on the left side. This concept was based on that of the Curitiba BRT model. However, during the construction of Phase 1 and after visits to Bogota, by the AMC and CEPT officials, it was decided to have an island type shelter with doors on both sides which would be a better choice. The intention of this decision was to reduce costs and allow easier transfers for passengers (AMC, AUDA, and CEPT University 2006–2012).

In Phase 1, all bus stops were close to the crossing points to allow faster downloads of perpendicular streets. However, with the provision of central bus media, passengers could not easily move from one stop to another bus that runs on the perpendicular road. In addition, providing overtaking lanes needed more space in the bus stop locations. This space was not available at many junctions and it also seriously compromised the mixed traffic, which required additional routes at intersections. Therefore, in Phase 2, it was decided to locate stops away from the junctions (CEPT 2006).

Shelters were designed to achieve a safe, simple and efficient passenger boarding and alighting. Platform level at the stations aligned with BRT vehicle floors so that boarding and alighting is smooth between the station and the vehicle. Different surface treatment with a gentle slope was done in areas between the mixed lane and BRT lane, to keep it user-friendly for differently abled commuters.

Access to Bus Stop

The plan was adequate to ensure the safe and comfortable movement of passengers back and forth from BRT bus stops. Pedestrian signals allowed safe passage of city dwellers guided through zebra crossings to reach the bus stops in the mid-block of RoW. To negotiate safely, the maximum number of mixed traffic lanes the pedestrians might cross is limited to only two at a time. At high volume bus stops, setting up an underpass for pedestrians to facilitate unlimited users who cross the BRT system was also planned. The bus stop near the intersections was accessible using the crosswalks at the intersection, followed by a gap of 2.0 meters between the BRT and the mixed traffic lane (CEPT 2006).

Treatment of Intersections

The proposal was to have a separate degree, installing the BRT system corridor in large intersections. Road space was planned with six track separators; two in the middle was dedicated to the BRT and two lanes on each side for mixed traffic except for BRT bus. However, in the flyover section, the reduction of physical separator between the mixed traffic and BRT before the flyover take-off point provided an extra width near the intersections under the bridge, and exploited in part to hold the buttress for the upper passage.

The design was to minimize conflicts and improve traffic flow in preference to BRT buses. The monitoring of all movements at intersections was by phased signaling. Traffic lights were programmed to allow safe passage of pedestrians and to regulate free left turn. Traffic in BRT bus route, mixed lane, bike lanes, operated only on signal that had overlapping or staggered phases for different lane movements of the same arm (CEPT 2006).

Parking Facilities

Corridors equal to or greater than 40 meters were equipped with a parking lane (3 meters) on both sides to meet existing parking demand. The parking lanes were integrated with the proposed service lanes and were physically separate from the mixed lanes. However, no parking was allowed 50 meters before and after each intersection. Instead, these lanes helped to provide additional passage lanes at intersections. A similar approach was followed in the case of spaces in front of an isolated half-stop; 100 meters of space was designated as no-parking from the isolated stops for parking any vehicles (CEPT 2006). In addition, provision for off-street parking facility was facilitated under the bridges wherever possible without compromising on safety regulations.

Cycle Paths

With respect to the relationship between the volumes of traffic in the bicycle corridors considered by the BRTS, proposed cycle paths had a minimum width of 2.0 meters on both sides of the road adjacent to the trajectory. In general, separation of cycle tracks was by a physical barrier from the main road, but here separation was by the difference in level of cycling track (20 centimeter) with a gentle slope, so that about 0.5 meters on both sides was saved (AMC, CEPT, Lea, and ITDP 2008).

Pedestrian Facilities

Pedestrian walking space was allocated a path of a minimum width of 2.0 meters on each side along the BRT corridor system. This facilitated the longitudinal movement of the urban population. Path level was higher by 20 centimeter on the cycle track with a gentle slope. Pedestrians other than BRT users also used the planned subways for crossings. For pedestrian crossings, it was recommended to have a crossing of 3 to 5 meters width in all arms at intersections.

Underground passages facilities were planned in places where the at-grade passage was dense to allow safe pedestrian movements without vehicular interventions. These underground pedestrian crossings were placed close to the bus stops, to offer better accessibility for pedestrians.

Street Lighting

Street lighting design was particularly important as it has to meet various lighting needs such as BRT buses operating in BRT lanes, other motorized vehicles in the mixed lane, motorized lanes and a pedestrian pathway. The lighting design must therefore cater to all these users, taking into consideration the basic design parameters of brightness, contrast, shielding, uniformity of light on sidewalks and aesthetics.

Street Furniture

Attention was given to the development of the corridor as a model road corridor; to not only meet the requirement for traffic in the express bus system but also to meet the needs of all urban users. In this regard, adequate furniture and support infrastructure were provisioned along the way, such as signs and traffic lights, road signs, railings, planters, toilets, cars and taxis, landfills, and so on.

Transfer of Existing Services/Utilities

Relocation of existing utilities such as telephone poles, electric poles, transformers, underground cables, water drainage, drainage pipes, and so on, were accommodated and if needed, effectively shifted to alternate locations and as underground utilities (CEPT 2006).

Operational Issues

Capability System

BRTS capability is a function of vehicle capacity, load factor, vehicle frequency and average vehicle speed. Based on the ridership estimate, the following parameters, in turn, affect the operational requirements in terms of the number of tracks, the supply of stations and terminals are set, and so on.

1. Bus capacity: 60 to 70
2. Load factor: 0.6
3. Peak frequency: 2 minutes
4. Off-peak frequency: 4 minutes
5. Waiting time: 20 to 40 seconds
6. Travel average speed: 30 kilometer per hour (AMC, AUDA, and CEPT University 2006–2012).

The proposal was to have 50 buses to start down a circular ring route covering about 58 kilometer long corridor in a closed system. Other 100 buses run at 5 to 6 radial feeders identified as a mixed system. The total size of fleet was expected to increase gradually to 1,000 over the next 10 years, as per the increase in demand. The plan was to build the first construction phase as a closed system in one circular channel system. In addition, there would be feeder corridors where the BRT buses operate in a mixed system with other state service such as AMTS and private vehicles. In later stages, some of these lines could be possibly converted as a closed BRT exclusive corridor system.

System Operation

In Phase 1, only one local service was planned and that stops at all stations. Then an express service was introduced that will not halt only at selected halt locations. Based on system performance, specific requirements that can arise in future, consideration of other services it was decided to revisit the decision on halt locations. Natural gas was decided as the operating fuel for buses and buses were designed with low floor. It was also decided to operate a mix of AC and non AC buses. Based on the approach adopted in Transmilenio, Bogota the allotment of offers for bus operators is after extensive discussions with the bus operators. The candidates selected to operate the buses have visited Bogota to hear firsthand the different best practices used by the operators there.

Fare Policy

Factors Determining Pricing Policy

The critical factors defining the transit pricing policy are:

1. The rate must be such that the system is accessible to most of the population, most of whom are in the lower middle-income category.
2. The rate must be high enough to maintain the system in good financial condition and preferably run with their incomes.
3. The rate should not be so high that passengers have another mode choice, which seems to be less expensive public transport.
4. Fraud control to the extent that the loss covers more than cost of leak testing.

The guiding principle was to use technology to reduce human error and the use of human resources to improve ease of use and detect revenue leakage. Automatic fare collection system (AFCS) was a step toward the realization of effective revenue management. Janmarg proposed to convert the full fare collection system overboard, preferably at the end of Phases 1 and 2.

Recovery Rate

The activity of collection of expenses is the collection of receipts and validation of means of travel. The following table summarizes the characteristics of each type of average rate.

Table 2.16 presents the comparison of various ticketing media and their distinct features.

Existing Tariff Structure

AMC wanted to seize the opportunity to implement BRT to complement the price structure for BRT and AMTS bus services. This was useful for all transit users. In the Ahmedabad Municipal transport system, division of costs can be observed in three main categories:

1. A single way ticket in distance: The starting price is Rs. 1 and up to Rs. 9.
2. Period: A daily pass is available for Rs. 20 that allows unlimited travel on all AMTS routes for one day. This pass is available for students and seniors at 50 percent discount.
3. Passenger pass: Monthly prepayment are given to general passengers who wish to benefit from a 50 percent discount for travel in the pre-registered round-trip area elected compared to the cost of what the regular daily tickets would cost for the same outward journey-back if purchased separately. Students receive a pass for Rs. 150/term (AMC, CEPT, Lea, and ITDP 2008).

Table 2.17 presents the percentage utilization of AMC Transport services as percentage revenue. Figure 2.10 illustrates the same.

Fifty seven percent travel is of single sector, which are with a one-day pass (8 percent of people buy a day ticket for unlimited trips and make an average of 4 trips/day). Another 4.3 percent of passengers spent the travel on monthly passes. Other forms of passes granted, most of which are students spend one semester in the form of 14 percent of the clientele. The 2008 revenue figures show that the average price per trip is Rs. 4.20, while the average rate for the entire trip in one direction is Rs.5.50.

Table 2.16 Ticketing media

Media type ↓ Features	Pre-printed tickets	Electronic paper tickets	Magnetic-stripe paper tickets	Smart card/smart token
Cost of media	Very cheap	Cheap	Medium cost	High
Cost of infrastructure	Very cheap	Medium	High	High
Revenue data collection/ compilation	Takes additional manpower and time (<1 week)	Real time/end of day	Real time/end of day	Real time/end of day
Verification	Takes time	Quick	Quick	Quick
Security	Low	Medium	Medium	High
Data security	–	–	Medium	High
On-board fare collection	Yes	Yes	Yes	Yes
Off-board fare collection	Not possible for distance based fare (high fraud)	Difficult for distance based fare for transfers	Possible for distance based fare and transfers	Possible for distance based fare and transfers

Source: AUDA and Gov. of Gujarat.

Table 2.17 AMC transport systems: Percentage revenue

Sr. No.	Ticket units	Percentage (%)
1	Single journey ticket trips	57
2	Day ticket journeys	25
3	Monthly pass	4
4	Student concession trips	11
5	Other	3

Amc transport system: division of cost

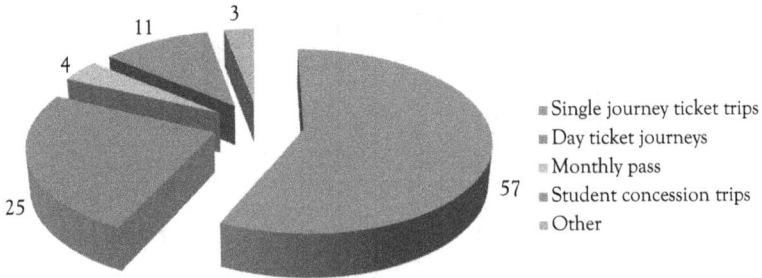

Figure 2.10 Percentage of various ticket units and the percentage of revenue from each type

Source: AUDA and Gov. of Gujarat.

Transfer survey conducted in February 2008 showed that just under 17 percent of passengers carry at least two or more trips to get to their destination (AMC, CEPT, Lea, and ITDP 2008).

Distribution travel in the denomination rate is shown in the previous table. The travel length is on average less than 8 kilometer. 42 percent of these trips are less than 5 kilometer long. It is interesting to note that riders who prefer to buy tickets for a trip make 60 percent of trips, but a one-day pass is available at quite cheaper price (Rs. 20/day for trips unlimited) (AMC, CEPT, Lea, and ITDP 2008). Any tariff structure must consider these statistics to retain the passenger.

Table 2.18 represents the AMC transport system distribution of travel in denomination rates (in INR) with percentage distribution among each denomination.

Table 2.18 AMC transport system: distribution of travel in denomination rates and figure 2.11 illustrates the same

Ticket denomination (INR)	Percentage (%)
1	9
2	14.5
3	19.5
4	16
5	14.5
6	11
7	11
8	3.5
9	1

To put all these passengers on public transport, it is important that BRT, AMTS passes and honor these multiple journeys. These two public transport regulators also share the revenue generated from these sources, 2008 statistics accounts for 39 percent of total revenue (AMC, CEPT, Lea, and ITDP 2008).

Passengers are very sensitive to rates. The sensitivity rate stems in the form of elasticity rate, defined as the percentage change in demand for a given percentage change in the rate.

The factors influencing the elasticity of the fare are as follows:

1. Quantum of fare changes: The higher the change in rate, the lesser the probability that passengers will be retained.
2. Competition from other modes: Strong competition from bus operators (such as AMTS) and means of transport such as cars, motorbikes will make more people sensitive to changes in interest rates.
3. Purpose of travel: Commuters traveling to work or school tend to be less sensitive to changes in interest rates, while tourists are more sensitive.
4. Distance: Passengers will be more sensitive to changes in rates if you travel over short distances because there are cheaper alternatives that can take them quickly to their destination.

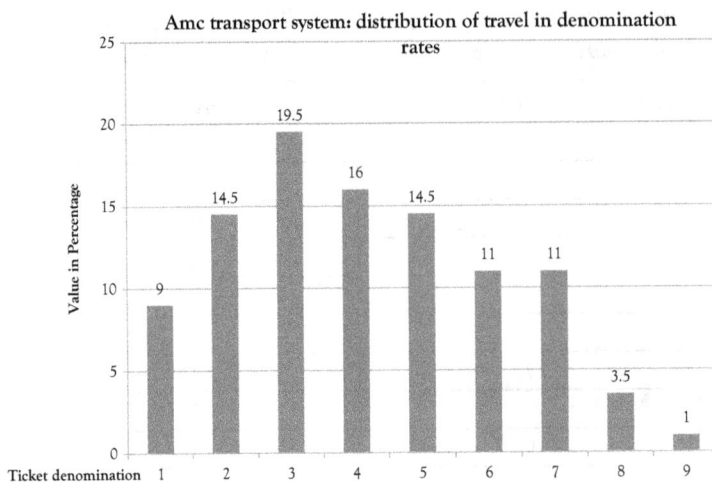

Figure 2.11 Distribution of Travel in Denomination rates

Source: AUDA and Gov. of Gujarat.

5. High versus OffPeak: Passengers tend to be less sensitive during peak periods, compared to off peak periods.

6. Income levels: Passengers with higher incomes are less likely to be sensitive to changes in interest rates than those with lower incomes.

7. Quality of service: Passengers may be less sensitive to fare changes if service quality is high (AMC, CEPT, Lea, and ITDP 2008).

A 15-minute wait for a short-stay bus ride would be equivalent to Rs. 2. This means that passengers are ready to take the fastest way by an auto[1] shared, even if it is twice as expensive as a bus ride. The average distance is 6.2 kilometer travel for a single trip. At the current average speed of 18.6 kilometer per hour bus, this results in a 20-minute journey (AMC, CEPT, Lea, and ITDP 2008). The average speed of the auto is slightly higher, resulting in a similar journey time, but with very little waiting time. Moreover, autos do also eliminate the end-mile connectivity issues of a commuter by providing an end-to-end mobility service. Therefore autos enjoy a higher patronage among the urban commuters in many

---

[1] A three-wheeler vehicle, that operates as an informal transit mode for short distances.

Indian cities, including Ahmedabad. It is estimated that about 350,000 daily trips are made by 3-seater and 7-seater auto-sharing in Ahmedabad. In percentage terms, this represents more than one third of all trips made on public transit. Autos are an important competitor for buses in some sections. They are the only means of transport in certain parts of the city. Therefore, the presence of autos cannot be ignored. In the physical design of major stations, adequate parking facility for autos was ensured for the rapid transfer of people, so that autos can serve as feeder services to BRT. At the same time, it is necessary to control the use of motor vehicles on the main arteries that are competing with buses.

Summary

Fare fixation policies may consider better discounts for group tickets and multi-trip tickets or cards. Such policies can potentially also reduce the time spent by ticketing staff. This is a form of positive price discrimination, which motivates a commuter who would otherwise choose another transit mode. Such policies have been successfully implemented in other countries to increase revenues and passenger numbers. BRTS should consider different alternatives and choose an appropriate mechanism and align the basic system design of the basic system and institutional arrangements.

Integration

Four types of system could work in different corridors of the city of Ahmedabad. These could be:

1. BRTS closed system
2. Mixed open system
3. AMTS open system
4. Rail system (in the future)

In the interest of public transit users, an integrated policy in place would ensure efficient transfer between systems in different corridors.

Evolution of Alternative Cross-Sections

The corridors identified for the BRTS called RoW proposed cross-sections. In urban areas, the existing line can hardly expand. When there is increase in traffic, space for safe pedestrian movement is as important as creating space for vehicular traffic. Therefore, the sections recommended at Phase 1 were based on not only the requirements of the BRTS, but also to accommodate the needs of other users of the corridor as of motorized traffic, cycles, pedestrians, and so on. The proposed improvement across the entire width of the road was expected to provide a better level of mobility in the corridor.

The preference or priority to provision space was to the pedestrians and cyclists throughout the project in places where there was a conflict between mixed traffic and pedestrians. Such an approach slows mixed traffic, thereby increasing their numbers of shorter mobility lanes to allow pedestrian movements. Provisioning parking space was the least priority and no parking space was provided wherever busway needed extra space for bus stops and lanes. As a result, there have been some changes in the design of Phase 2 based on the experience gained during the implementation of Phase 1 and learning from other cities. The most important change is the elimination of electric light poles from the bus median and shifting its location to the sides to allow a better visibility for the BRTS drivers. The width of the footbridge increased slightly to 2.3 meters from 2 meters and to 2.6 meters in some cases, while the width of the bicycle path increased to 2.4 meters (AMC, AUDA, and CEPT University 2006–2012),(AMC, CEPT, Lea, and ITDP 2008). Brief discussions on RoW at different sections follow:

RoW (60 meters)

Centralized lanes for bidirectional bus width of 7.5 meters (as compared to 7 meters in Phase 1); one for each direction will replace the existing median. Separator of 1.75 meters width for mixed traffic lane will face these. There will be three motorized routes for mixed traffic for each direction of travel. A 2.5 meters wide bicycle path running alongside the mixed traffic lane secured by a 0.25 meters separator. A 3.75 meters next

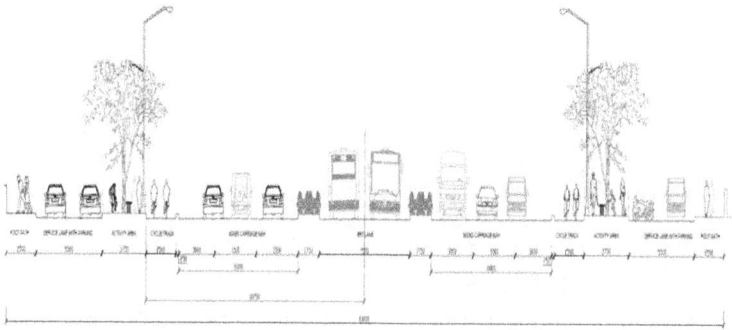

Figure 2.12 CS A-A: *Cross-section of the BRT bus station system (60 meter)*

Source: AMC and AUDA.

to the cycle path, will facilitate activities such as itinerant sales, utilities, landscape, and so on. A service track 5.5 meters wide (7 meters in Phase 1) on both sides was planned to allow vehicle traffic origins and destinations in the corridor to move. Outside, there would be a 2.5 meters wide lane footpath for each direction of travel. The Figure 2.12 illustrates the 60 meters RoW road cross-section.

Wherever there are large sections available at mid-block or intersections, they are to provide emergency/storage lanes, landfills, public washrooms and landscaping in general. Access to adjacent properties and streets will be limited to service lane. These traffic will join the motorized crossings or specific locations. The purpose of having a trajectory of 1.75 meter wide footpaths, next to the BRT track is to accommodate without abomasa stops and, in the future will create a BRT system taking three lanes 1.5 meter from without changing the entire length of the road (AMC, CEPT, Lea, and ITDP 2008).

RoW (40 meter)

Centralized lanes for bidirectional bus width of 7.5 meters (7 meters in Phase 1); one for each direction will replace the existing median. Separator of 0.75 meters width (1 meter in Phase 1) on each side will face these. Mixed traffic lanes are 8.5 meters wide for each direction of travel. 2.1 meters wide (2 meters in step 1) was proposed parking on the street. A 2.4

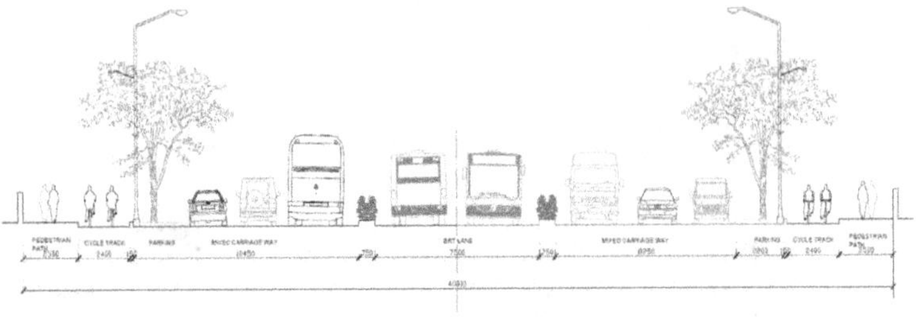

Figure 2.13 CS B-B: *Cross-section of the BRT bus station system (40 meters)*

Source: AMC and AUDA.

meters wide runway for cycle will run adjacent to the parking area with a 0.15 meter separator between the two. It offers a 2.35 meters wide foot-bridge (2.0 meters in stage 1) along the roadside (AMC, CEPT, Lea, and ITDP 2008). This will address the movement of pedestrians and access to land and adjacent activities on the road. Whenever there is additional width in the intermediate block at intersections or sections, it is to provide emergency/storage lanes, landfills, public toilets and landscape in general. Access to adjacent properties and streets will be limited to motorized lane. Parking is limited in such location. Figure 2.13 illustrates a 40 meter road cross-section.

RoW (36 meters)

Centralized lanes for bidirectional bus width of 7.5 meters (7 meters to Phase 1). Mixed traffic lanes 6.25 meters wide that extends along the bus lane separator with a median width of 0.75 meter between them were proposed. Along the route, an unseparated cycle track of 2.25 meters (2 meters in stage 1) was proposed. Parking is 2.3 meters wide next to it, followed by 2.7 meters wide pavement. Therefore, the most important development after Phase 1 was the increase in the width of the pedestrian walkway from 2.25 meters in Phase 1 to 2.7 meters (AMC, CEPT, Lea, and ITDP 2008). Wherever there are large sections available at mid-block or intersections, it was to provide emergency/storage lanes, landfills, public washrooms and landscaping in general. Service lanes will directly feed

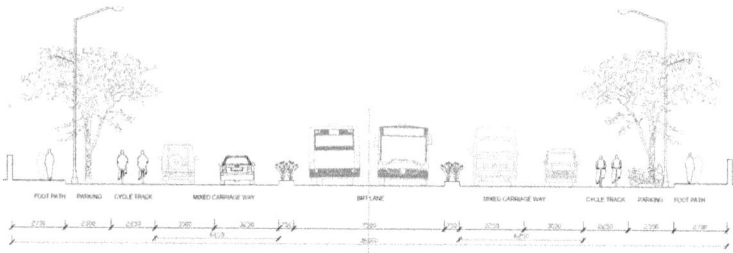

Figure 2.14 CS C-C: *Cross-section of the BRT bus station system (36 meters)*

Source: AMC and AUDA.

access to adjacent properties and streets. Parking was limited in such locations. Figure 2.14 illustrates a 36 metre road cross-section.

RoW (30 meters)

Centralized lanes for bidirectional bus width of 7.3 meters (7 meters in step 1) were proposed. The following is a width of the mixed track of 6.0 meters on both sides of BRT tracks with a median width of 0.75 meter between them. There was a 2.1 meters long car parking along the mixed lanes. For pedestrians, installation of 2.5 meters pedestrian promenade on the road edge (AMC, CEPT, Lea, and ITDP 2008) was also proposed. The mixed roads ensured the access of the vehicles within the available land space. Tree holes were located in parking spaces in every 12 to 18 meters depending on local conditions. The mounting of street lamps in this bay was designed to keep minimum obstruction to pedestrian way. Figure 2.15 illustrates a 30 meter road cross-section.

RoW (24 meters)

In 24 meters RoW, the design must be receivable from the available width. Bus routes of two wide lanes of 7.3 meters each were in the middle. A carriageway of 5.5 meters wide was proposed on either side of BRT bays with a separator of 0.75 meter. There was no provision for on-street parking. A large pedestrian promenade of 2.5 meters by the side of the

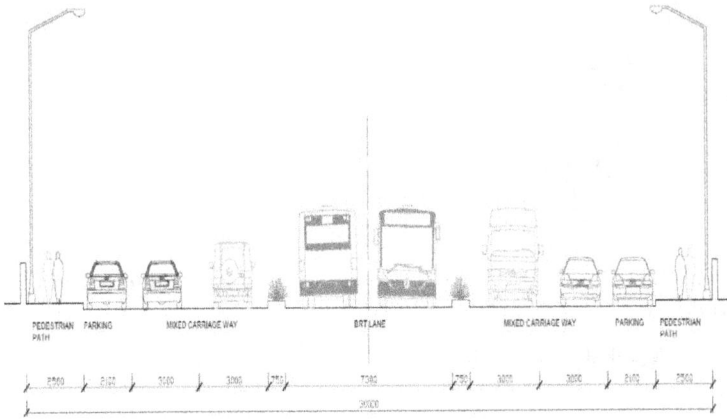

Figure 2.15 CS D-D: *Cross-section of the BRT bus station system (30 meters)*

Source: AMC and AUDA.

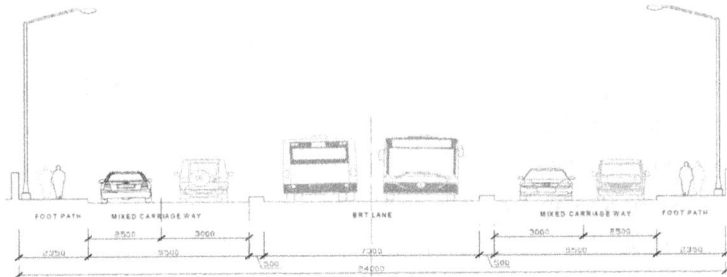

Figure 2.16 CS E-E: *cross-section of the BRT bus station system (24 meters)*

Source: AMC and AUDA.

road (AMC, CEPT, Lea, and ITDP 2008) was proposed. Figure 2.16 illustrates a 24 meter road cross-section.

Overtaking Lanes

Requirement of Overtaking Lanes

Proposal of overtaking lanes was to allow for greater capacity of bus operations. Overtaking lanes allow for express planning routes, which halt at the main destinations and not at all bus station. Providing overtaking routes reduced chances of congestion during peak hours, by allowing vehicles to run at their free-flow speed in an uninterrupted manner.

In Phase 1, there were no overtaking paths. Indeed, the demand in certain corridors was not high enough to justify an overtaking path. However, in Phase 2, the proposal was to develop the radial access to the city and with the estimated demand over the next five years, it was imperative to have overtaking pathways in certain sections wherever possible in the RoW.

Drawing Basics

It is difficult to accommodate overtaking lanes in few routes, where the two directional paths were parallel to each other due to width constraints. Therefore, in such locations, based on the division of stops for both directions, it was decided to accommodate the overtaking lane at the bus stops. An additional track width of 3.5 meters was provisioned at the stop to serve as overtaking lane for traffic in either direction. At such stops, division of passages was planned based on the inward and outward movement of commuters. The Figure 2.17 shows the basic layout for overtaking lanes (AMC, CEPT, Lea, and ITDP 2008).

Cost Estimates

The total revenue sanctioned for the Phase 1 of BRTS was about Rs. 493crores for a length of 58.3 kilometers, and as part of Phase 2, it

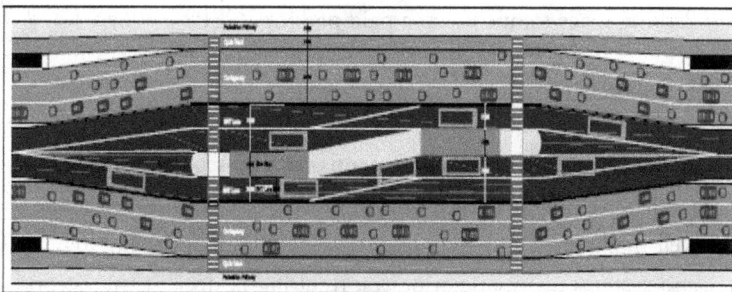

Figure 2.17 Overtaking lanes in a typical cross-sectional area of 40 meters

Source: AUDA and Gov. of Gujarat.

was proposed to develop 30.5 kilometers of BRT corridors. Total development cost of corridors covering decommissioning, road works, paving and concrete, road signs, signals and marking, street furniture, landscaping, electricity, and so on, was estimated. The total cost with a five percent scaling for corridor development was Rs. 49,387 lakh (4.9 Bn) (AMC, CEPT, Lea, and ITDP 2008). The year marked fund allocation by different stakeholders is presented in Table 2.19.

Economic Evaluation

Ahmedabad BRTS was a multi-faceted project plan that integrated land use and transportation, various forms of transit services, including other motorized and non-motorized modes through various physical, operational and political interventions for achieving a smooth urban mobility in Ahmedabad. Given this multidimensional nature of the project, it is anticipated that urban mobility in Ahmedabad will significantly improve in terms of measurable and qualitative outcomes.

The BRT project in Ahmedabad comprises a 155 kilometer gradation of the road network of divided roads in progress/undivided partially developed, open to mixed traffic in a fully planned road with the following facets:

1. The physical separation area for buses, bicycles, pedestrians and mixed traffic,
2. Lighting and other adequate operational infrastructure on the street,
3. Services to road users, such as toilets, kiosks, telephone, and so on,
4. Parking space to operate as a paid parking (CEPT 2006).

The following benefits are also expected:

1. **Increase in public transit patronage:** The regular bus operations tend to worsen after a certain number of years, unless systems and well-maintained and upgraded. The operational costs tend to increase and systems quality deteriorates, resulting in decrease in patronage, and increasing operational cost. As a result, it is likely that only the captive riders continue to use the buses, with increasing levels of dissatisfaction. Combined with improving life styles and spending

Table 2.19 Project funding pattern

Agency	Percentage	Year 1 (in INR)	Year 2 (in INR)	Year 3 (in INR)	Amount (in INR)
AMC	50	976,269,999	732,202,500	732,202,500	2,440,674,998
GoG	15	292,881,000	219,660,750	219,660,750	732,202,500
GoI-JUNNURM	35	683,389,000	512,541,750	512,541,750	1,708,472,499
Total	100	1,952,539,998	1,464,404,999	1,464,404,999	4,881,349,997
Percentage		40	30	30	100

Source: AUDA and Gov. of Gujarat.

power, urban population aspires to shift their daily commuting on owned vehicles. All these lead to low ridership, which lead to significant losses for the state operators. It is eluded as a discouragement to additional investment in purchases and modernization, and is classically termed as the low-level balance trap. To make urban transport sustainable, it is necessary to improve the quality of services by providing modern transit options in fair prices, that is, operating with a customer focus.

2. **Effective public transit operations:** BRTS operations can become more efficient, if processes are simplified and operations are made customer centric and sustainable. Utilization of vehicles and infrastructure should be higher with increased vehicle speed, so that throughput time is short but more numbers of trips are run. Labor costs can be reduced by off-board ticketing, and improving labor utilization and productivity. Operating costs must also be reduced by better maintenance, improving fuel efficiency and reducing beakdowns.

3. **The reduction of accidents:** BRT corridors are very prone to accidents. By proper traffic segregation, exclusive pedestrian and bicycle tracks, better lighting, and stringent regulation, accidents on these roads are likely to fall by 75 to 90 percent (AMC, CEPT, Lea, and ITDP 2008).

4. **Improved air quality:** The BRT benefits in terms of improved air quality are due to shifting to high occupancy buses from higher number of less occupancy personal vehicles, cleaner fuel adopted by BRTS, promoting non-motorized mobility and integration of bicycles and pedestrian structures.

In addition, private sector investments in the purchase and operation of buses, efficiency gains are likely to be expected. General traffic management in the city would improve, leading to better air quality and less pollution.

Financial Analysis

Project Costs: Costs include road construction, infrastructure related to BRTS, pedestrian facilities, and so on, as well as operation and

Table 2.20 Summary of economic and financial analysis

Projection from 2006 to 2026	
Economic IRR without value of time (EIRR)	34.5%
Financial IRR with value of time (FIRR)	49.8%
Financial internal rate of return (FIRR)	2.72%

Source: Ministry of Urban Development, Government of India.

maintenance. In addition, maintenance costs including BRTS control room operations, demand assessment, monitoring services costs, would be recurring expenses.

Project Revenue: Project revenue streams include:

1. Net income from pay and park facilities
2. Advertising revenue along the way
3. Advertising revenue on buses and related facilities
4. Expenditure for subcontracted activities, such as ticketing systems, subscriptions, and so on.

The Table 2.20 presents the details of estimated costs and benefit flows and the estimated financial internal rate of return (FIRR). With limited options for direct cost recovery, FIRR is very low. However, socio-economic benefit, which translates into high economic rate of return (EIRR), is quite high, making the project economically viable. (AMC, AUDA, and CEPT University, City Development Plan Ahmedabad 2006–2012).

Implementation Strategy

AMC has been extensively involved in developing physical infrastructure and other essential elements of BRT, such as hiring and bus shelter, terminals, storage and BRT workshop. The municipal commissioner headed the project implementation team with support from the deputy city commissioner in daily monitoring and field inspections. A resident engineer AMC, solely responsible for the BRTS project worked closely with the project management consultant, LEA Associates, to complete the road infrastructure. The University of CEPT supported by LEA Associates and the Institute for Transportation and Development Policy has led the design consultants (AMC, CEPT, Lea, and ITDP 2008).

Summary

To ensure greater mobility in the identified corridor as a whole, they provided separate cyclist and pedestrian tracks, motorized lanes and BRT bus lanes. Various sections were explored to integrate separate and mixed circulation of traffic, bicycle and pedestrian paths for RoW availability. Bus shelters were placed strategically and were planned to allow the overtaking of buses and other vehicles.

Challenges in Implementing Ahmedabad BRTS

Urban planning for the city of Ahmedabad was developed exclusively based on land transportation and poor land use planning that led to random urban sprawl, traffic congestion and air contamination. Existing structures further hindered planning and development of BRTS. Boundary conditions for the BRTS implementation in Ahmedabad are as follows:

Insufficient Demand

Urban expansion is often a characteristic of cities growing rapidly in the development of Asia that indicates a lack of effective planning and uncontrollable growth over several years.

Ahmedabad BRTS Has Failed to Reduce the Use of Private Vehicles

BRTS Ahmedabad, administered by Ahmedabad Janmarg Limited (AJL), had minimal impact on the use of private vehicles, according to a UN Environment Programme (UNEP). According to the study, while only 12 percent of BRTS travelers have switched from private vehicles, more than 45 percent moved from AMTS. In addition, while private vehicles increased by 10 to 12 percent year-on-year; the number of BRTS monthly users has remained more or less stagnant at 130,000 to 132,000 over the past two years (Umarji 2016).

After the project replaced its routes in AMTS buses and autos, 47 percent of public transport users went to BRTS and only 13 percent from the share of users through the autos. Only 12 percent of travelers moved from private motor vehicles. However, only 42 percent of users have taken the BRTS for more than 21 days in a month (Umarji 2016). This means that the BRTS is still unable to earn a sustained passenger ship in the city. Through this study, it is also found that the BRTS had not been able to reach low-income groups as it served mainly middle-income groups, most of whom were captive users of longer-distance public transport.

According to AJL, despite the launch of several recent initiatives like BRT buses for women and special discounts for the use of smart cards for BRTS travel by way of promotions, price sensitive traits among the citizens do not still endorse BRTS. The city traffic has a daily addition rate of about 600 new private vehicles. In addition, travelers are very price sensitive and service quality conscious. The pay back of any decline in fuel prices is in the form of increased use of private vehicles and vice versa. In addition, to encourage more private vehicle users to opt for BRTS, attempts are made to provide BRT ticket holders free of charge parking space for their private vehicles.

Of the total number of users, only 13.7 percent belong to families with incomes up to Rs. 5,000. 62.2 percent of users had a monthly income of more than 10,000 rupees. This is despite the fact that a large number of low-income dwellings and the fall of slums within 500 meters, or nearby the BRTS network. Meanwhile, the average number of passengers in Ahmedabad BRTS remains a concern. The daily number of passengers per day at Ahmedabad BRTS has increased from 25,000 in 2009 and 50,000 in 2010 to a maximum of 135,000 in 2011 before reducing to 125,000 in 2013. As in December 2015, it increased to 132,000 passengers per day (Umarji 2016).

The 12 percent BRTS ridership is also considered a huge number. BRT buses run on the roads less frequently than AMTS, therefore, each transit operator has different passenger growth rate. In fact, there is need to get more people switch to BRTS and the city must continually look for new ways to market public transport, and certainly BRTS holds substantial potential as a high quality urban mobility choice. BRTS is one of the transit modes introduced by the state to reduce the number of private vehicles on the road and to help solve air pollution in Ahmedabad.

The popular daily newspaper DNA has conducted a two-part series on Janmarg based on the results of a study conducted by two researchers at the CEPT University. The researchers found that Janmarg was not attracting the tributary section of the society, but it is also too expensive for low-income groups. It had also failed to reduce pollution levels in the city, as people who use private vehicles did not make the switch. Complaints against BRTS are now familiar as well, such as lack of space for pedestrians, cycle lanes and other vehicular movements.

At the present rate of addition of new vehicles on city roads, traffic congestion would increase. However, improvement of many roads was due to BRTS, which had benefited other traffic as well. It has helped reduce the carbon footprint of 1.25 lakh passengers per day. The pollution level has decreased considerably because of multiple transit systems and better coordination between them.

When compared on fare structure, the city has the lowest fares of all major cities in India. The ticket price for the shortest stage of Ahmedabad BRTS is Rs. 3 and it increases with distance. The minimum price for regular bus services in Delhi and Mumbai are Rs. 5 (Niyati Rana 2012).

Official figures indicate that BRTS covering 89 kilometers reduced the city's total transit public use of nearly 18 percent. It is interesting to note that the vehicle population of the city increased to 25.10 lakh in 2015 that is, 54 percent from 18.2 lakh in 2009 during the existence of BRTS. According to officials of the AMC, before the existence of BRTS, public passenger traffic is about 8.5 lakh per day (John 2016). Today, combined passenger traffic of BRTS and AMTS fell to 7.5 lakh passengers per day, which beat the very purpose of the BRTS.

Operational Difficulties BRT

With poor initial planning of the city, city plans do not include transit systems of the urban road network, resulting in huge challenges in developing an integrated urban structure. Many roads grew on their own—too narrow and congested for multiple stakeholders, especially during peak hours. Therefore, a good plan is necessary for the BRT system busway, especially in the construction of the busway road surfaces on existing roads. Priority installation at the intersection of traffic lights is another issue that requires a good design of the system (SATIENNAM, FUKUDA, and OSHIMA 2006).

In the case where the design of a BRT corridor is to transmit an intersection with high volumes of traffic, design of road signaling system should give priority to the BRT bus and at the same time reduce the traffic flow from other approaches. At intersections with a slight delay, this signal priority system may not be necessary. However, for the actual implementation of the BRT system, detailed planning of the operational performance of the BRT and its impact on the traffic is required.

One of the main problems in the BRTS corridor is related to street parking, where most of the footpaths and service roads have become unauthorized parking lots. In many places, vehicles are parked on roads obstructing the circulation of traffic, and are the cause for accidents. According to a survey conducted by RITES, about 80 percent of road traffic delay is due to street parking.

Poor implementation of the BRTS: Bus corridor of Bogota BRT has a 4-lanes and 6-lanes for motor vehicles, whereas Ahmedabad has two lanes for buses and 4-lanes for cars. Reduced road space has resulted in major fatal accidents. In addition, motor vehicles ply on cycle lanes. Following are few drawbacks in the implementation of Ahmedabad BRTS:

1. Modification of the layout to reflect the concerns of NHAIs,
2. The presence of the subsoil hampered work during construction,
3. Price escalations due to rise in prices of steel and cement,
4. The cost-effectiveness of operational deficiencies,
5. Poor response from bus manufacturers (Valoriser).

Inadequacy of BRT Presentation in Public Transit System

In most developing countries in Asia, BRTS is considered as an innovative urban transportation mode. Awareness about BRTS among urban citizen might be poor; as they cannot distinguish between the normal bus system and the BRTS. As a result, the bus system seems still unattractive, mainly because their development requires the conversion of an existing lane into an exclusive bus lane; private vehicle users have negative attitudes, which can cause more congestion along the BRT corridor.

In comparison with successful BRT's across the globe, the factors that could hinder the development of BRT in Ahmedabad are:

1. Land-use patterns: Urban sprawl, which leads to a low population density that extends throughout the city;
2. Existing road networks in the city: There is no room for the development of traffic congestion line but the traffic congestion is serious. Just by implementing a BRTS and to hope that it would resolve the entire city's traffic related issues is unrealistic and inappropriate. Development strategies of the BRT system would possible support a smooth urban mobility (SATIENNAM, FUKUDA, and OSHIMA 2006).

Summary

Dedicated Right of Way

Ideal: Dedicated BRT tracks lead to congestions in other vehicular pathways; by applying delineators or color flooring.
Fact: BRT had a lane reserved for buses.

Alignment of Bus Bay

Ideal: Median aligned bus bays to minimize the risk of delays caused by rotational movements and parked vehicles.
Fact: Ahmedabad BRT has been right in its approach, by developing a bus bay is in the center.

Off-Board Fare Collection

Ideal: The off board collection reduces loading time, and prevents revenue leakage.
Reality: Ahmedabad has yet to automate all their collection rates in the bus system.

Intersection

Ideal: Preventing turns across bus routes and simplifying signal cycles reduce delays. Priority traffic signal would accelerate BRT vehicle movements.

Reality: Traffic signals were long in some directions, but had no impact. Jams continued on the crossing.

Boarding Platform

Ideal: The floor of the bus and the platform of the station must be at same level.
Fact: The levels are the same, but the passengers had no connection to the sidewalks, to cross the traffic to get to the bus stop.

Insights and Way Forward

Before embarking on further expansion of BRTS corridors, the following considerations are important:

1. The right corridor with a reasonably high demand for public transport service must be chosen.
2. Space for BRT lanes must be allocated right at the beginning while planning new developments.
3. Movements of other types of vehicles and private cars should be restricted in narrow roads.
4. Last mile connectivity should be provisioned wherever necessary and possible, as it makes BRTS very attractive for commuters.
5. Dedicated spaces should be provided for pedestrians and cyclists.

References

AMC, A.M., A.U. AUDA, and A. CEPT University. 2006–2012. *City Development Plan Ahmedabad.* Ahmedabad: JnNURM.

AMC, A.M., U. CEPT, A. Lea, and ITDP. 2008. *Bus Rapid Transit System, Ahmedabad.* Ahmedabad: Ministry of Urban Development.

CDP. 2006–2012. *City Development Plan.* Ahmedabad.

CEPT, U. 2006. Ahmedabad Bus Rapid Transit System (ART): Working Paper-1, Vehicle Technology, p. 84.

CEPT, U. 2006. Ahmedabad Bus Rapid Transit System (ART): Working Paper-3, Road Utilities, p. 67.

CEPT, U. 2006. Ahmedabad Bus Rapid Transit System (ART): Working Paper-4, Bus Station Design, p. 41.

CEPT, U. 2006. Ahmedabad Bus Rapid Transit System (ART): Working Paper-5, Traffic Volume Characteristics, p. 18.

CEPT, U. 2006. Ahmedabad Bus Rapid Transit System (ART): Working Paper-6, Land Use Restructuring, p. 36.

CEPT, U. 2006. Ahmedabad Bus Rapid Transit System (ART): Working Paper-9, Environment Impact Assessment, p. 37.

CEPT/GIDB. 2005. *Ahmedabad BRTS Report No. 1.*

Mahadevia, D., and R. Joshi. November 30, 2013. "Ahmedabad's BRT System: A Sustainable Urban Transport Panacea?" *Economic and Political Weekly*, pp. 56–64.

JHA, B.K. July 14, 2012. "One of the Major Problems on BRTS Corridor is on Road Parking, Most of the Footpaths and Service Roads have Turned into Parking Zone. At Many Places Vehicles are Being Parked on the Road As Well Obstructing Flow of Traffic and Causing Accidents." According. *Times of India*, p. 1.

John, P. January 1, 2016. "In Era of BRTS, Users of Public Transport Shrink." *Times of India*, p. 1.

NIUA, N.I. 2014. *Urban Transport Initiatives in India: Best Practices in PPP.* INDIA Waste Management Portal.

Rana. N. October 10, 2012. "BRTS Will Do Better with Metro in Ahmedabad." *DNA India*, p. 1.

Patel, D.M. *Fact File—A Complete Ahmedabad City Guide.*

Satiennam, T., A. Fukuda, and R. Oshima. 2006. *A Study on the Introduction of Bus Rapid Transit System in Asian Developing Cities*, p. 11.

Umarji, V. January 20, 2016. "Ahmedabad BRTS Fails to Bring Down Use of Private Vehicles." *Business Standard*, p. 1.

Valoriser, C. Challenges. India.

Google Images.

www.brtdata.org/location/asia/india/ahmedabad

http://narendramodi.in

http://ahmedabad.com

http://ahmedabadbrts.com

http://welcometoahmedabad.com

http://wikipedia.com

CHAPTER 3

Delhi Metro Rail Corporation

Introduction

For the first time in history, more people live in the urban areas than in the rural areas. The defining trait of urban areas is density: of people, activities and goods. Since these cities contribute substantially to a country's gross domestic product (GDP), growth and development, they require high quality infrastructure systems to facilitate the movement of people, goods and delivery of basic services to people. However, developing such systems is a complex endeavor and can be challenging for any government. The solution should involve aspects relating to funding, management, maintenance and efficient operation of services, which are also environmentally sustainable. Growing cities and their population have called for a major improvement in the transport network, demanding a shift from private modes of conveyance to public transport systems.

Urban Mobility in India

(a) **Urbanization**

Urbanization patterns present huge challenges to urban mobility systems. In 1951, there were only five Indian cities with a population greater than one million and 42 cities with a population greater than 0.1 million; much of India effectively lived in villages. In 2011, there were 468 cities with a population of above 0.1 million and 53 cities with a population greater than 1 million. Population distribution in the Indian cities is presented in Table 3.1.

Table 3.1 Number of cities as per population (Census 2011)

Population	Number of cities
>10 million	3
5–10 million	5
2–5 million	10
1–2 million	35
0.5–1 million	43
0.1–0.5 million	372
Total no. of cities	468

Between 2001 and 2011, India's urban population increased from 286 million to 377 million and is expected to be 600 million by the year 2031, which constitutes almost 40 percent of the total population of the country. In the coming years, cities and towns are expected to become the major contributors of Indian economic growth.

(b) **Rapid growth in private vehicles**

Since 2001, the number of private owned vehicles in Indian metropolitan cities has increased significantly. Five metro cities have vehicle registrations of over 500 per 1,000 people. In 2011, Delhi (1.4 percent of Indian population) had the highest vehicle population with almost 6.3 million registered vehicles, constituting 5 percent of all motor vehicles of the country. Table 3.2 illustrates the decennial growth in number of vehicles in India.

(c) **Decreasing share of non-motorized transportation**

Non-motorized transportation or active transportation includes cycling, walking and other variants. As cities grow, the share of non-motorized vehicle reduces drastically and there is an increase in private vehicle ownership. Non-motorized transport modes are usually slow and inhibit the speed of travel in cities. The poor in a city are the ones who walk and cycle, but badly constructed footpaths, no cycle tracks and poor maintenance of road infrastructure restricts their usage.

These urban mobility trends have resulted in urban transport problems of road congestion, parking, air pollution and deteriorating road

Table 3.2 Growth of registered vehicles in India

Year	Number of vehicles
1951	0.3 million
1961	0.7 million
1971	1.9 million
1981	5.4 million
1991	21.4 million
2001	55.0 million
2011	141.8 million

Source: Road Transport Yearbook (2009–2010 and 2010–2011), MoRT & H, Government of India

safety in all the major metropolitan cities of the country. In the case of our capital city Delhi, vehicular pollution started deteriorating from 1990 as the growth of vehicles outpaced population growth and economic development. While the number of vehicles grew by 87 percent to 3.6 million between 1990 and 2001, the city's population increased by a mere 14 percent from 9.5 to 13.8 million in the same period.

Delhi-Background

Delhi is known to have been inhabited since 6th century BC. It is also widely believed to have been the legendary capital of the Pandavas. It has a strong historical background owing to the fact that it was ruled over by some of the most powerful emperors in Indian history. The history of the city dates back to the time of the Mahabharata when it was known as Indraprastha. The other kings occupied and developed cities like Lalkot, Siri, Dinpanah, Quila Rai Pithora, Ferozabad, Jahanpanah, Tughlakabad and Sahajahanabad. The present city of Delhi was founded in the 17th century by Mughal Emperor Shahajahan with a population of about one lakh. This area is now known as old Delhi. In the year 1857, the city came under British rule. The British shifted their capital from Calcutta to Delhi in 1911. It is the city of many ancient and medieval monuments and archaeological structures. It was made a Union Territory in 1956. Lying in the northern part of the country, Delhi is surrounded by Haryana on all sides except the east, where it borders with Uttar Pradesh.

The 69th Constitutional amendment is a milestone in Delhi's history, as it got a Legislative Assembly with the enactment of the National Capital Territory Act, 1991. New Delhi houses important offices of the Federal Government, including the Parliament of India, as well as numerous national museums, monuments, and art galleries. The National Capital Region (NCR) in India is a name for the conurbation or metropolitan area which encompasses the entire National Capital Territory of Delhi as well as urban areas ringing it in the neighboring states of Haryana, Uttar Pradesh, and Rajasthan. The National Capital Territory of Delhi lies central to the NCR. It includes the city of Delhi and New Delhi. This region has the largest concentration of population in the whole of the NCR.

Delhi, the capital of India is the largest metropolis by area and the second-largest metropolis by population in India. It is the eighth largest metropolis in the world by population. According to the 2001 census, the population of Delhi, as on March 1, 2001, was 13.85 million as against 9.42 million on March 1, 1991. The corresponding percentage at the all-India level was 21.34 percent. During the years 1901 to 1911, the decennial growth of Delhi was 11.13 percent, which increased to 106.58 percent in 1941 to 1951. From then on, it steadily decreased. The decennial growth reduced to 46.87 percent in 1981 to 1991. However in 1991 to 2001, it rose to 52.34 percent.

The Northwest and South districts are the most populated districts in Delhi with a population of 2.847 million and 2.258 million, respectively. However Northeast, Central and East are densely populated with 29,395, 25,760, and 22,637 people per km², respectively. According to Census 2001, the density of population in Delhi is 9,294 persons per km² as against 6,352 persons in 1991. The density of population at the all-India level was 324 persons per km² in 2001. The density of population in Delhi is the highest in the country.

Decennial growth in absolute values and percentage growth of Delhi population is presented in Table 3.3.

Delhi is well connected by roads, rail and air with all parts of India. It has three airports—Indira Gandhi International (IGI) Airport for international flights, Palam Airport for domestic air services and Safdarjung Airport for training purposes. It has three important railway stations—Delhi Junction, New Delhi Railway Station, and Nizamuddin Railway

Table 3.3 Population of Delhi

Year	Population	Decennial Growth (%)
1901	4,05,819	–
1911	4,13,851	11.13
1921	4,88,452	27.94
1931	6,36,246	46.98
1941	9,17,939	55.48
1951	17,44,072	106.58
1961	26,58,612	64.17
1971	40,65,698	54.57
1981	62,20,406	58.16
1991	94,20,644	46.87
2001	1,38,50,507	52.34

Source: Economic Survey of Delhi 2001–2002

Table 3.4 Registered vehicles in Delhi

Year	Private vehicles	Commercial vehicles	Total vehicles
2002–2003	3,732,481	207,928	3,940,409
2003–2004	3,980,422	222,033	4,202,455
2004–2005	4,275,642	232,384	4,508,026
2005–2006	4,529,177	279,833	4,809,010
2006–2007	4,889,710	295,700	5,185,410
2007–2008	5,307,894	319,490	5,627,384
2008–2009	5,657,313	354,418	6,011,731
2009–2010	6,068,909	382,974	6,451,883
2010–2011	6,454,232	390,295	6,844,527

Source: EIA for Phase three corridors of Delhi Metro (RITES)

Station. Delhi has three inter-state bus terminals at Kashmiri Gate, Sarai Kale Khan, and Anand Vihar. The vehicle population in Delhi is the highest among all metropolitan cities (Bombay, Calcutta, Delhi, and Madras). As on February 2011, there were 6,844,527 private and commercial vehicles registered in Delhi. The annual increase in different types of registered vehicles in Delhi can be observed in Table 3.4.

Need for a Mass Rapid Transit System in Delhi

The population of the capital city started increasing dramatically after partition and the population doubled from 0.6 million to 1.2 million in 1947 itself. With Delhi's population reaching around 3.5 million in 1970, the need for a mass transportation system was evident. The Central Road Research Institute (CRRI) conducted a study in 1971 and recommended mass rapid transit system (MRTS) on two corridors, with one feeder connection to the ring railway line, covering 51.3 km. Another study in 1975 by the Metropolitan Transport Organization (MTO) of the railways recommended a service network of 97 km and an underground network of 36 km by 1981. A number of studies were performed on having a rail based system, but these studies remained on paper and did not become a reality. The only Metro existing in India at that time was in Kolkata, built and controlled by the Indian Railways, under the Ministry of Railways. It involved a cost overrun of 12 times the project cost and a long gestation period of 16 years and also disrupted city life very badly. So, in 1986 the subject of Metro Rail type transport was transferred from the Ministry of Railways to the Ministry of Urban Development.

It was finally in 1989 that the Government of Delhi realized that buses alone would not be able to carry the forecast traffic, and thus decided to engage Rail India Technical and Economic Service (RITES), a Government of India PSU under the Ministry of Railways to undertake a Detailed Project Report (DPR) to have a rail based transport system in Delhi. The DPR was completed in 1994, and was forwarded to the Ministry of Urban Development.

The DPR had the following features:

- Delhi's population in 1991 was 9.3 million. Buses catered to about five million commuter trips per day. This was expected to rise to 11.4 million trips per day by 2001.
- In the absence of an MRTS, the number of motorized vehicles went up from 1.8 lakh in 1971 to 25.4 lakh in 1995. Of these, about 66 percent were two-wheelers, highlighting the need for a more workable form of public transport.

Even at the DPR preparation stage, the total number of vehicles in Delhi was more than the total number of vehicles in Mumbai, Chennai, and Kolkata combined.

- An LTR system would not suit Delhi's requirement because its capacity would be only 25,000 PHPDT, so an MRTS was needed.
- Of the total atmospheric pollution in Delhi, about 75 percent was estimated to come from automobile exhaust. The average vehicle speed on Delhi roads was in the range of 15 to 18 kmph. More than 10,000 casualties were reported in 1993 on Delhi roads, resulting in one of the highest accident rates for Delhi.
- The transport demand forecasting was done on the basis of detailed household surveys, speed and delay studies, limitation of road capacity, and so on.

The DPR suggested a 184.5 km MRTS network covering the entire National Capital Territory (NCR) region, including planned extensions like Najafgarh, Rohini, Dwarka, and so on. A 55.3 km stretch was approved as Phase-I covering Delhi University-Central Secretariat, Shahdara-Barwala and Sabzi Mandi-Holambi Kalan.

The project was ultimately approved by the Government of India (GoI). The loan from the Japan Bank of International Cooperation (JBIC) was formalized and approved in 1995. The Cabinet approval for the project was received on May 3, 1995 and the Delhi Metro Rail Corporation Ltd. was registered as a company with 50 percent equity participation from the Government of National Capital Territory of Delhi (GNCTD) and 50 percent from the GoI.

The Birth of Delhi Metro Rail Corporation

The unique Joint Venture company was created, with no government holding majority shares in the company, as both had equal participation and equal equities. The Board of Directors of the company consisted of five representatives from the GoI and five from the Government of Delhi, with the Chairman of the company being appointed by the GoI, while the Managing Director was to be appointed by the Government of Delhi.

The Ministry of Urban Development then appointed P.K Gupta as the Assistant Company Secretary and he joined as the first employee of the company on April 4, 1997. The construction of the Phase-I could not begin several months after the DMRC and JBIC signed the loan agreement as the search committee wasn't able find a suitable candidate for the position of Managing Director to head the project and DMRC. There was immense pressure on GNCTD to get the project started, as JBIC had given the ultimatum that they would withdraw the loan if a Managing Director was not appointed by October 1997.

Dr. E. Shreedharan, who was then Chairman and Managing Director of Konkan Railway Corporation was recommended for the position of Managing Director by P.V. Jai Krishna, the then Chief Secretary of Delhi. Unfortunately, he was already 65 years old and had passed the accepted retirement age of 58. He had retired at the age of 58 as member, Engineering from the Railway Board in 1990 after which he took over as the CMD of the Konkan Railway Project, which was going on at that time. As a compromise, Dr. Shreedharan was asked to assist in the selection of the Managing Director of the DMRC by the then Chief Minister of Delhi, Sahib Singh Verma, Lieutenant Governor, Tejendra Khanna and Transport Minister of Delhi, Rajendra Gupta. Much to Dr. Shreedharan's surprise, they requested him to head DMRC as the Managing Director and the meeting ended with him being appointed as the MD. Khanna assured him that all the hurdles would be taken care of; all they needed was his commitment to undertake the position. However, Dr. Shreedharan had a few conditions—that he would be allowed to build his own organization, there would be no bureaucratic or political interference in the working of DMRC and he would be given complete powers to make decisions for the company. Initially, from August 1997 to November 1997, he played a dual role, by looking after the Konkan Railway project at Mumbai and informally looking after the affairs of DMRC. It was finally in November 1997 that he took over as the Managing Director of DMRC. All the powers of the Board of Directors were vested in him, with the exceptions of certain powers that the Indian company law prevented from being delegable.

Implementation

Phase-I

In principle, approval was accorded by the GoI in July 1994 to go ahead with the multimodal MRTS for Delhi covering a distance of 184.5 km with an estimated cost of INR 75 Billion at 1992–1993 prices. The first phase of 67.5 km was estimated to cost Rs. 3,401 crore. While the DPR was initiated as per this decision, the actual project approved in September 1996 was for a 55.3 km Phase-I at a cost of INR 48 Billion. Some changes were considered necessary during implementation, which were approved by the GoI in August 2000 and July 2002. The total cost of Phase-I was modified to Rs. 10,571 crore in December 2002. The project was originally scheduled to be completed by September 2005 but the date was revised to December 2005 due to delays in land acquisition for the Barakhamba Road-Connaught Place-Dwarka corridor.

A review of the Phase-I corridors was undertaken by DMRC. This showed that there had been no development in the area through which the Rithala-Barwala (6 km) would pass and the development of the area to generate commuter traffic would take at least a decade. So, a proposal to replace the Rithala-Barwala section with the Barakhamba Road-Indraprastha section was initiated by DMRC in September 2003. This section which would yield higher ridership, with 80,000 additional passengers a day, was preferred.

The Delhi Development Authority (DDA) approached DMRC in 2003 with the proposal to extend the Barakhamba Road-Connaught Place-Dwarka corridor to Dwarka Sub-city for almost 6.5 km. The DDA committed to provide land free of cost both for DMRC and people who would be rehabilitated. Earlier DDA had earmarked a 30 meters wide stretch of land for an LRTS to connect Dwarka Sub-city but DMRC advised DDA that a standalone network would not be the correct selection, as an LRTS with a small length with different system parameters would have cost implications. So, DMRC took the decision to extend the Barakhamba Road-Dwarka corridor to Dwarka sub-city. The two extensions were approved and commissioned. Subsequently, there was a cost revision of Phase-I and completion cost was fixed at Rs 10,571 crore. Tables 3.5 and 3.6 present implementation and modification details of phase 1 of DMRC.

Table 3.5 Implementation of Phase-I (DMRC)

Route	Section	Date of commencement
Line 1 Shahdara-Rithala (22.06 km)	Shahdara-Tis Hazari Tis Hazari-Inderlok Inderlok-Rithala	December 24, 2002 October 3, 2003 March 31, 2004
Line 2 Vishwavidyalaya-Central Secretariat (10.84 km)	Vishwavidyalaya-Kashmiri Gate Kashmiri Gate-Central Secretariat	December 20, 2004 July 3, 2005
Line 3 Barakhamba Road-Kirti Nagar-Dwarka (25.65 km) Extension of Line 3	Barakhamba Road-Kirti Nagar Dwarka-Dwarka Sub-city Barakhamba Road-In-draprasta	December 31, 2005 April 1, 2006 November 11, 2006

Table 3.6 Modifications of phase-I (DMRC)

Route	Changes
Vishwavidyalaya-Central Secretariat-ISBT-Central Secretariat	Instead of 11 km underground, 10.84 km was to be constructed underground
Shahdara-ISBT-Trinagar-Nangloi	Modified as Shahdara-Trinagar-Barwala, with 27.84 km in place instead of the earlier 25 km
Sabzi Mandi-Holambi Kalan	Modified as Barakhamba Road-Connaught Place-Dwarka with a total length of 22.9 km (with 1.12 km underground) in place of 19.4 km

Thus, the project execution of Phase-I commenced on October 1, 1998 and was completed by December 31, 2005 within the approved cost and two years and nine months before the deadline. The total length of Phase-I was 65.10 km.

Phase-II

With Phase-I making progress, the Phase-II proposal was actively taken up. A notable feature of the second phase of the Delhi Metro was that additional corridors were also taken up from time to time. The funding plan for phase 1 of DMRC is illustrated in Figure 3.1.

Funding plan for phase-1

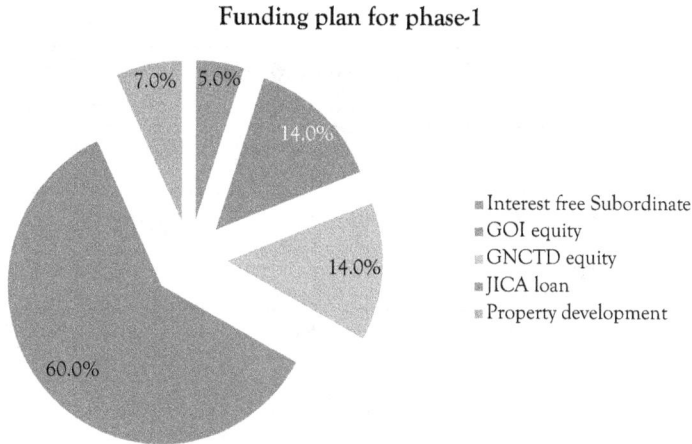

Figure 3.1 Funding plan for Phase-I (DMRC)

Source: Total cost of completion: INR 105.71 million.

An extension from Ambedkar Colony to Sushant Lok in Gurgaon was approved on October 17, 2006. The total length estimated was 14.47 km (7.42 km in Delhi and 7.05 km in Haryana). The entire route was planned to be elevated and the cost estimated was INR 15.81 millions including central tax and duties, which was revised to Rs. 15.89 billion in March 2009 for shifting of entry and exit points and providing escalators at the metro station in Gurgaon. This was the first extension of the Delhi Metro to Haryana.

The Central Secretariat-Badarpur corridor (20.16 km) was approved on October 17, 2006. It aimed at providing connectivity between the Jawaharlal Nehru Stadium and Dr. Karni Singh Shooting Range at Tughlaqabad for the Commonwealth games scheduled for October 2010 and was commissioned just in time for the Commonwealth Games. The completion cost was estimated at Rs. 4,012 crore including central taxes. Implementation details of Phase II of DMRC is presented in Table 3.7.

A high speed express link from New Delhi Railway Station to the IGI Airport was approved on December 21, 2006. The total length was to be 19.2 km and the estimated cost was Rs. 3,076 crore including taxes. Of this route, 15.13 km was to be made underground and the remaining portion was to be elevated/at grade. This was a Public-Private Partnership

Table 3.7 Implementation of phase-II (DMRC)

Route	Length (in km) and elevation type	Date of commencement
Vishwavidyalaya-Jahangirpuri	6.36 km (0.94 underground and 5.42 elevated)	February 4, 2009
Central Secretariat-Qutub Minar	12.53 km (11.76 underground and 0.77 elevated)	September 3, 2010
Shahdara-Dilshad Garden	3.09 km (all elevated)	June 4, 2008
Indraprastha-New Ashok Nagar	8.07 km (6.07 elevated and 2 at grade)	May 10, 2009/May 13, 2010
Yamuna Vihar-Anand Vihar ISBT	6.17 km (all elevated)	January 2010
Anand Vihar-Vaishali	2.5 km	July 14, 2011
KIrti Nagar-Ashok Park	3.31 km (all elevated)	August 27, 2011
Inderlok-Mundka (SG)	15.15 km (all elevated)	April 3, 2010

(PPP) arrangement between DMRC, Reliance Energy and CAF.[1] It was scheduled for completion in September 2010 but could be made operational only in February 2011.

The extension of the airport express link from IGI Airport to Dwarka Sector 21 was approved by the GoI on January 18, 2008. It comprised a completely underground 3.5 km standard gauge at an estimated completion cost of INR 79.3 billion including central taxes. It was scheduled for completion in September 2010 but became operational with the commencement of the Airport line.

The extension from New Ashok Nagar in Delhi to Sec 32, Noida was approved on January 18, 2008. This seven km elevated stretch had an estimated cost of INR 82.7 billion and was commissioned in November 2009.

Thus, for the first time, Delhi Metro was able to establish connectivity with a prominent town in NCR. The Metro Railways Amendment Act, 2009 provided an enabling provision for the legal cover of the metro operation in NCR (as well as metropolitan cities and metropolitan areas in the

---

[1] Spanish Rail infrastructure manufacturing company.

Funding plan for phase-2

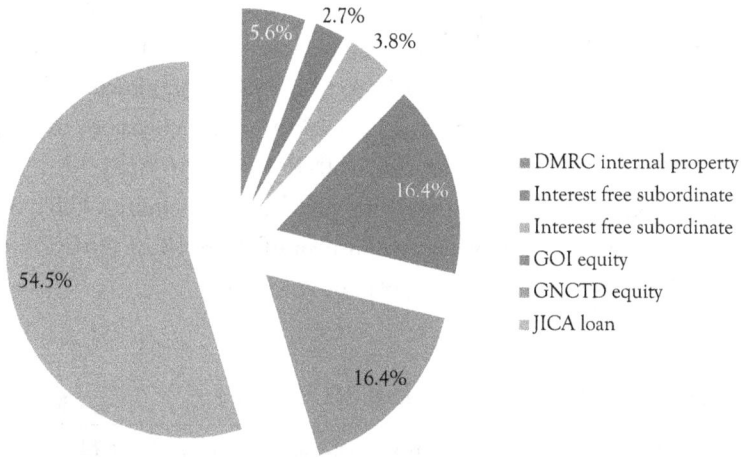

Figure 3.2 Funding plan for Phase-II (DMRC)

Source: Total cost of completion: Rs. 19.258 crore.

country) under the Metro Railways (Construction of Works) Act, 1978 and the Delhi Metro Railway (Operations and Management) Act, 2002.

Extension of the metro link from Dwarka Sector 9 to Dwarka sector 21, fully elevated, with a length of 2.76 km was approved in January 2008 at an estimated completion cost of INR 35.6 Billion including central taxes. It was commissioned in September 2010.

The entire Phase-II network other than the subsequent additions was completed by October 2010, thereby providing good connectivity to travelers during the October 2010 Commonwealth Games. The total length was 121.62 km and the completion cost was fixed at INR 0.19 Trillion, as illustrated in the funding plan of Figure 3.2.

Phase-III

After the immense success and the recognition of the first two phases of Delhi Metro, planning for Phase-III started with the deadline for completion fixed as 2016. However, it is now expected that the entire Phase III will only be completed by 2018. For the first time Delhi Metro, the construction of ring lines were planned in Phase III. Till Phase II, Delhi

Metro had focused on expanding the reach of the metro and thus built long radial lines. However, in Phase III, DMRC aimed to interconnect existing lines through ring lines to improve connectivity. The aim was not only to reduce distances but also to relieve radial lines of some congestion.

Out of the two new lines and 11 route extensions proposed for Phase III, the cabinet approved two new lines and 10 route extensions totaling 167.27 km, with an estimated cost of INR 41,079. In April 2014, the Delhi Lt. Governor gave approval for two further extensions. Table 3.8 has the details of the implementation plan of Phase III of DMRC and Figure 3.3 illustrates the funding plan of Phase III.

Table 3.8 Implementation of phase-III (DMRC)

Route	Length (in km) and elevation type	Date of commencement
Majlis Park-Shiv Vihar	58.596 km (39.479 km elevated and 19.117 km underground)	Expected-September 2017
Janakpuri West-Kalindi Kunj	34.273 km (10.466 km elevated and 23.807 km underground)	Expected-June 2017
Central Secretariat-Kashmere Gate	9.370 km (all underground)	June 26, 2014
Jahangirpuri-Samaypur Badli	4.373 km (all elevated)	November 10, 2015
Badarpur-Escorts Mujesar	13.875 km (all elevated)	September 6, 2016
Dwarka-Najafgarh	4.295 km (2.754 km elevated and 1.541 km underground)	Expected-December 2018
Mundka-Bahadurgarh	11.182 km (all elevated)	Expected-December 2017
Dilshad Garden-Ghaziabad Bus Adda	9.41 km (all elevated)	Expected-April 2018
Extension of Metro to Ballabhgarh	3.2 km (all elevated)	Expected-June 2018
Kalindikunj to Botanical Garden	3.962 km (all elevated)	Expected-June 2017
Extension of Metro from Noida 32-Noida 62	6.675 km (all elevated)	Expected-March 2018

Funding plan for phase-3

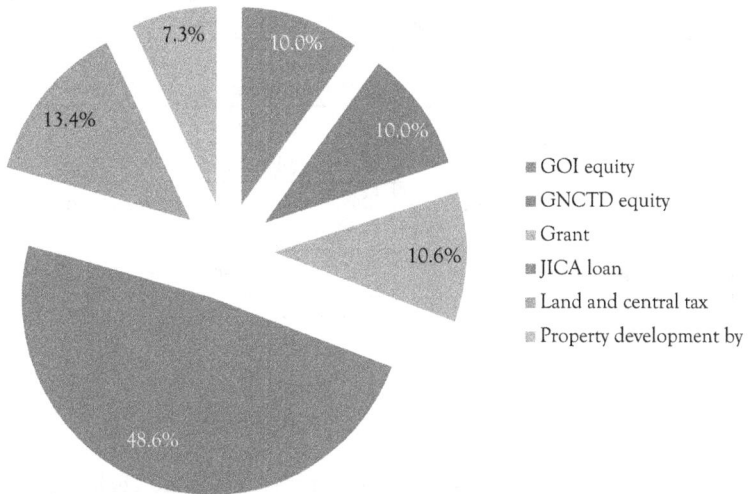

Figure 3.3 Estimated funding plan for Phase-III (DMRC)

Source: Total estimated cost of completion: Rs. 41,079 crore.

Phase-IV

DMRC proposed Phase-IV, with an estimated length of 104 km to boost connectivity to the Capital's outskirts, the airport and south Delhi. Phase IV has a 2022 deadline, and tentatively includes further extensions to Sonia Vihar, Burari, Mukundpur, Reola Khanpur, Palam, Najafgarh, Narela, Ghazipur, Noida sector 62, extensions of Violet line, Green line, and Line 8. Details are presented in Table 3.9.

The project was approved by the Delhi Government's Cabinet in January 2017 and has since then been waiting for the Central Government's approval. There is still no confirmation on its funding split and which external agency is going to provide a loan to fund it. Meanwhile, consultants are currently conducting various pre-construction surveys, such as geotechnical investigations, topographical surveys and soon a hydro-geological study. Data captured from these activities will help prepare detailed designs, cost-estimates, and will be included in the tender documents whenever the DMRC invites civil construction bids.

Table 3.9 Proposed implementation plan for phase-IV (DMRC)

Route	Length (in km) and elevation type
Rithala-Bawana-Narela	21.73 km (all elevated)
R.K. Ashram-Janakpuri (west)	28.92 km (7.74 km underground and 21.18 km elevated)
Mukundpur-Burari-Maujpur	12.54 km (all elevated)
Inderlok-Delhi Gate-Indraprastha	12.58 km (all underground)
Aerocity-Saket-Tughlakabad	20.20 km (14.62 km underground and 5.58 km elevated)
Lajpat Nagar-Chirag Delhi-Saket G block	7.96 km (2.07 km underground and 5.89 km elevated)

Overcoming Challenges

The initial years of DMRC were filled with obstacles and challenges. At the time of DMRC's incorporation, the only existing Metro in India was the 25.14 km long Kolkata Metro. However, the first phase of Kolkata Metro had taken 23 years to construct with a cost overrun of 12 times. The construction caused immense disruption and inconvenience to the lives of residents of Kolkata, and when it finally started, the technology was already outdated and almost 25 years behind the technology used by Metro systems around the world. So DMRC, not having an example to follow, had to start at the bottom of the learning curve, overcoming several hurdles to build its reputation and deliver an excellent MRTS to the residents of Delhi.

Appointment of General Consultants

After DMRC's basic organizational structure was put in place, it was decided to establish its own technical capabilities in order to ensure that the Metro network was up to international standards. To achieve this, tenders were called by DMRC for appointment of General Consultants. The bidding started out with the submission of six tenders, but soon the bidders had formed into three consortia for which DMRC evaluated technical and financial bids. DMRC then started the negotiations with the consortium that had the highest ranked bid, comprising Pacific

Consultants International (PCI), Parsons Brinkerhoff International (PBI), Japan Railway Technical Service (JARTS), Tonichi Engineering Consultants and RITES. Although the cost of the contract was estimated at close to Rs. 4 billion, the final contract was awarded at Rs. 2 billion, and a provisional letter of acceptance was issued in June 1998 to the selected agency. PCI were also the in-house consultants for the JBIC which gave the major loans to DMRC, so this led to speculation in the media about whether the appointment had been completely open and transparent. The government took up the matter for an in-depth examination, but Dr. Shreedharan stood by his decision and openly disclosed details to clarify the process of bidding and appointment on several occasions. The government finally cleared the selection process and a newspaper that had printed the incorrect information, issued a public apology.

Deciding Upon the Railway Gauge

Several important technical decisions were to be taken before the construction of the Metro lines could begin, and one of the most crucial decisions DMRC had to take was whether to use broad gauge or standard gauge for the Metro in Delhi. In 1999, almost 90 percent of Metro networks across the world used standard gauge as it provided better speed, maneuverability and safety, while also allowing for sharper and therefore space saving turns on the tracks. However, the Ministry of Railways (Railway Board) was in favor of adopting the broad gauge, in keeping with the "unigauge" policy of India. It felt that adopting broad gauge would facilitate inter-connectivity of rolling stock between the Rail and Metro networks. Dr. Shreedharan felt that inter-running of trains between the Metro and railway tracks was not feasible. After 18 months of discussions and debate, the situation reached a point where Dr. Shreedharan could either continue to lock horns with the Ministry of Railways and risk further delay, or accept the Ministry's demand. He chose the latter course of action though on the night of August 4, 2000, when the Group of Ministers declared the final decision to use broad gauge, he was tempted to resign, but was dissuaded from doing so by Vijai Kapoor, the Lieutenant Governor of Delhi. Over time, he persuaded the Ministry to reverse its stand and use standard gauge for the upcoming lines. Almost 61.4 km of

Phase-II tracks used Standard gauge and the entire Phase-III network of DMRC was planned on standard gauge. Unfortunately, due to the use of different gauges, interchangeability of stock within the two phases of the Metro remains a problem.

Technology

The Delhi Metro was being built from 1998 onwards, therefore the company had an option of either going in for an old and conventional Metro System or they could adopt the latest technical features from the new metros such as Singapore and Hong Kong.

DMRC decided to take advantage of the fact that had entered the field of Metro technology very late, and thus took the decision to adopt extremely modern air conditioned rolling stock with Automated Train protection and Automatic Train Operations system rather than the conventional suburban trains, which provided a high level of safety by ensuring safe train separation and increased productivity of rolling stock by increasing line capacity and train speeds. Terrestrial trunk radio (TERTA) was adopted to ensure trouble free communication and DMRC became the first metro to adopt 25 kV rigid over head electrical (OHE) systems for an underground Metro. A paperless ticketless system was adopted with the AFC system of DMRC being the most advanced since it was the first metro to have contactless tokens for single journeys. DMRC used the near field communication (NFC) technology which allowed the exit machines to read/write data on the tokens. Retractable flap type control gates were used, which offered high throughput, required less maintenance and were the latest internationally. Contactless smart cards were also introduced for multiple journeys, replacing the need to buy a token for every single journey. It was decided that the Delhi Metro should run on advanced ballast less track, thus minimizing the need for track maintenance and long welded rails ensuring that track joints are minimized, providing more riding comfort and reduced noise levels.

The Legal Framework

As DMRC was ready to start its day-to-day operations, they found to their surprise that there was no legal cover for the project. This left the entire project exposed to all types of legal issues and potential litigation, which could slow down the progress on the construction of the remaining lines and make the operation of the Metro rail system difficult. As the Prime Minister of India was set to inaugurate the Metro line on December 24, 2002, an ordinance was promulgated two months before the inauguration, and subsequently the Delhi Metro Operations and Maintenance Act was passed during the next session of Parliament.

The Act granted the Metro administration four main powers:

- To acquire, hold and dispose of all kinds of properties owned by it, both movable and immovable;
- To improve, develop or alter any property or asset held by it;
- To develop any Metro railway land for commercial use;
- To execute any lease or grant any license in respect of the property held by it.

Among various other things, the Act provided for the constitution of a Fare Fixation Committee and the appointment of a Commissioner of Metro Railway Safety. The Fare Fixation Committee ensured that Metro fares would be fixed on realistic lines as the committee was headed by a High Court judge and would not be decided based on populist requirements. The Commissioner for Metro Railway Safety was necessary as without safety clearance, the Metro system could not be made operational and open for public use. The Act was amended to the Metro Railway Maintenance and Operations Act, 2002 in 2009 to permit the Central Government to extend the Act to any metropolitan city or area, after consultation with the concerned State Government.

Tax Concessions

DMRC had requested import and excise duty concessions for the equipment and rolling stock imported by the organization; however neither the GoI, nor the Government of Delhi provided any tax exemption to it during the initial stages of the project. However, once the first line was completed before the scheduled deadline, and the Government was convinced that DMRC would be able to deliver the Metro on time, it agreed to grant the Delhi Metro project customs and excise duty concessions amounting to Rs. 14.07 billion in 2002. In addition, the Government of Delhi waived sales tax and works contract tax to the extent of Rs. 3.93 billion. Both the Central and State Governments provided several other tax concessions as the project progressed in Phase-I and Phase-II.

Difficulty in Land Acquisition and Realignment

A large number of people who were affected due to the proposed alignment of Metro routes (Project Affected Persons or PAPs) protested against some of the planned routes and demanded the realignment of the routes. One of the controversial areas was the Metro line near an area where a large section of the legal fraternity had their offices near Kashmiri Gate/ Tis Hazari. Unhappy about the fact that they would have to relocate their offices, a group of lawyers called for a meeting to discuss the issue with the Chief Minister of Delhi, Sheila Dikshit, who supported the DMRC. She came out openly and stated that experts proficient in their job had planned the alignment, and she would do everything in her power to help those who had faced any inconvenience, but realignment was out of the question. DMRC subsequently faced a number of such alignment issues and always tried to minimize disruption to the daily lives of people living in nearby areas, without having to alter their technical plans and strategies.

DMRC used a similar approach while dealing with the land acquisition issues. According to the laws, the government could legally acquire private land needed for development projects by suitably compensating the landowner. But DMRC officials and workers made personal visits and engaged with the landowners, ensuring that the land was handed over to the DMRC without too many problems. The need for private land acquisition was kept to the minimum while planning the Metro alignment. Dr. Shreedharan paid personal attention to these issues, which helped curb any mutinous tendencies, thereby avoiding costly and time consuming litigation in a number of cases.

The shifting of religious structures is a sensitive issue in India. Small temples and idols were encountered a number of times near the Metro alignment and neglecting them could have created controversies and harmed the image of DMRC. But DMRC relocated all these with

DMRC engineers holding direct discussions with the temple priests, assuring them that the original temples would be shifted brick by brick to the new locations by Metro construction engineers.

In a particular instance, the government needed to rehabilitate approximately 300 shopkeepers near Shahdara before DMRC could use the land. Instead of waiting for the relevant government department to work out where and how they would settle the shopkeepers, DMRC after discussing with the affected persons, bought land close by, constructed shops and provided this to the displaced traders at a nominal price.

The Land Acquisition, Rehabilitation and Resettlement Act, 2013 came into force from January 1, 2014. On December 31, 2014, the President of India promulgated an ordinance with an official mandate to "meet the twin objectives of farmer welfare; along with expeditiously meeting the strategic and developmental needs of the country." With no mechanism to implement the new Land Acquisition Ordinance, the Delhi Metro, in its Phase III project, lagged behind schedule for the first time since its inception. DMRC had to reach out to private owners of land to settle acquisition, one of the major reasons DMRC missed its 2016 deadline for the completion of Phase-III.

Underground Tunneling Challenges

Almost 20 percent of Phase-I covering 13.17 km of line was built entirely underground. At Chawri Bazar, the entire station was built inside an underground tunnel at a depth of 25 meters. The tunnel boring method (TBM) was used by the construction contractors initially, to dig around the Nayi Sadak area in old Delhi while connecting Delhi main to Chawri Bazar. However, the cutting head of the Tunnel Boring Machine could not cut through the rocks and broke, thus leading to several delays. DMRC extended the contractor's deadline by several months and brought in new machinery, but the project could not progress further due to the hard and abrasive nature of the rocks in that area. Finally after a lot of push from DMRC, the contractors switched to the new Austrian Tunneling Method from the opposite end in order to complete the tunneling within the assigned deadline. The construction team faced several challenges like water seepage in the tunnel and had to reconfigure their entire approach.

Dr. Shreedharan's goodwill and quick decision making skills, allowed DMRC to convince the contractors to proceed along the new approach and complete the section by the target date. Had DMRC waited to renegotiate the construction contracts, it may not have been able to operationalize the line within the allocated time of two years. This was accomplished without disturbing the over ground heritage and historical surface of Chawri Bazar which had many old structures from the Mughal era.

Crisis Management

DMRC had faced number of crisis situations since the organization began functioning effectively in 1997. The crash of the launcher at the Laxmi Nagar construction site on October 19, 2008 in which two people were killed and nine were injured, followed by another crash of a launcher on July 12, 2009 at Zamrudpur in which seven people were killed and 15 injured left DMRC's image and employee morale cruelly shaken. These were, in fact, the first structural collapses that took place since DMRC began its construction activities.

There had been a total of 100 deaths in the first two phases of Delhi Metro, but most of these accidents were caused due to mistakes such as a person coming in the way of some construction machine or slipping at the site. There had been no situation where a structure came falling down, till the Laxmi Nagar case in 2008. In the first instance, DMRC was able to effectively deal with the crisis. They quickly briefed the press about the accident and took quick steps to remove the debris from the site.

In the Zamrudpur case, the Metro convened a Press Conference within a couple of hours of the accident on July 12, 2009, in which a prepared statement was read out giving the basic facts of the event which had happened. These details included, the type of accident, the number of people killed and injured, their names and the names of hospitals they had been shifted to, including details of the interim compensation. Another press conference was convened at 3 p.m. on the same day, where Dr. Shreedharan announced his resignation in view of the accident. This led to a huge furor in the press and in the city with the Chief Minister insisting that Dr. Shreedharan withdraw his resignation. Ultimately, he was persuaded to withdraw his resignation.

It was very unfortunate for DMRC when on July 13, the next day, one of the huge 400 ton cranes, which was working simultaneously to lift the collapsed launching grinder failed, and all the cranes came toppling down one after the other, resulting in massive chaos at the site. The TV crews and media persons were filming the recovery operations at the time of this incident and not only did they have a narrow escape, but their cameras were also able to capture the cranes live, which was telecast immediately. This did irreparable damage to the Metro's image of being an efficient organization, which it had built over the past decade's hard and dedicated work. The chief engineer (Design), Rajan Kataria and the deputy chief engineers were suspended.

With the release of the Inquiry Committee's report, a somber mood had settled over the DMRC office. From their investigation, the committee had found that deficiencies in both design and material had caused the grinder to collapse.

It took almost one year for DMRC to emerge from this situation. This period was the most difficult time that the DMRC faced, in handling the press and external pressure groups during the entire Phase-I and Phase-II. However, public support still continued to be with DMRC, as they were very happy with the metro services being provided to them. Dr. Shreedharan regained the public trust and re-motivated his workforce to quickly get the project back on track.

Public Private Partnership—The Airport Line

Metro projects are very expensive and are social. They are not expected to make profits. Private players will come in only when there is profit. Personally, I do not favor the PPP model for metro projects. Ideally, it should be a 50:50 participation from Central and state governments. Therefore, no particular government can dominate.

—Dr. E. Shreedharan, Managing Director, DMRC

DMRC's Phase-I and Phase-II were widely regarded as a success. Patronage was somewhat lower than expected, but was sufficient to make Delhi one of the few metro systems in the world that did not need operating subsidies.

Travelling by air in India grew rapidly from the year 2000. As a result, roads leading to airports in major metropolitan cities in India became heavily congested. Delhi experienced particularly rapid growth in air traffic. A few city line buses which stopped at the airport *en route* to and from other destinations were the only public transport services to Delhi Airport.

Delhi was awarded the 2010 Commonwealth Games, a major event that would see a large influx of competitors, spectators and media to the city, most of whom would arrive through the airport. Recognizing the increasing traffic to the airport, DMRC proposed to build a dedicated and high speed metro line to the airport. The journey between New Delhi Railway Station and the airport, which would normally take two hours by road due to traffic congestion, was expected to get reduced to just 18 minutes.

DMRC had built and operated the first two phases of the metro system itself. In contrast, it decided to offer the airport line as a PPP to a private concessionaire to build the line and operate it for a period of 35 years. As the cost of building the airport line was high, the concessionaire would not be able to recover the full capital and operating costs of the project from fares alone. Therefore, DMRC proposed to undertake all the civil works itself, including the viaduct, the tunnels and the stations. The private concessionaire would be responsible for financing only the operating systems—primarily the track, signals, power distribution system and rolling stock—and for paying operating expenses.

The procurement of the concessionaire was based on a two stage competitive bid. Criteria for eligibility included a financial profile of bidding consortia, and prior experience of developing or operating or maintaining rail based urban transport systems or as a major equipment supplier for a rail based urban transport system.

Delhi Airport Metro Express Private Limited (DAMEPL)—an SPV formed between Reliance Infrastructure Ltd. of India and Constructions y Auxiliar de Ferrocarriles, S.A. (CAF) of Spain was awarded the contract in January 2008, on the basis of their highest quote for annual concession fees to be paid to DMRC. Reliance Infrastructure Ltd. held a 95 percent stake in DAMEPL, with the remaining 5 percent being held by the Spanish firm.

The project was to be completed in 30 months by July 31, 2010 before the Commonwealth Games. DMRC gave a one month extension to the August 31, 2010 deadline for the commencement of operations. However, a two day inspection in September found out that false ceiling, emergency staircases and exit points, ticket counters, electrification work, software and signaling were incomplete, for which DMRC demanded compensation. Operations commenced on February 23, 2011, with four of the six stations operational.

The express link was shut down for six months in July 2012, when the operator pointed out the cracks that had developed on its metro pillar structures. The private partner claimed damages for losses due to closure of the line and also tried to exit the project citing financial non-viability. However, in January 2013, the line was reopened with a reduced speed limit of 50 km per hour, as compared to the earlier speed of 105 km per hour.

In August 2012, Reliance Infrastructure transferred 65 percent of its stake in DAMEPL to associate companies of the Anil Dhirubhai Ambani Group without consulting DMRC. The blame game started between DMRC and DAMEPL and as problems mounted and became irreconcilable, DAMEPL's principal sponsor, Reliance Infrastructure, bailed out. DMRC took over the operations of the line with effect from July 1, 2013.

Management Strategies

Steady Leadership—The Metro Man

Dr. E Shreedharan was born in 1932 in Palakkad district of Kerala. He studied at Victoria College in Palakkad and later completed his Civil Engineering from the Government Engineering College, Kakinada. From there he went on to work as a lecturer in Civil Engineering at Government Polytechnic, Kozhikode for a short tenure and worked as an apprentice at the Bombay Port Trust for a year. He cleared the ESE-1953 conducted by UPSC and joined the Indian Engineering Services (IES). According to him, the Railways, being the most challenging and prestigious, was the first choice for any bright engineer back then and he was no different.

In 1964, a tidal wave washed away a large portion of the Pamban bridge linking Mandapam and Rameshwaram in Tamil Nadu. The state government fixed a target of six months for restoring the bridge. The Railways brought this deadline down to three months and put Dr. Shreedharan in charge of the project. Under his supervision, the project was completed in just 46 days. He made a reputation for himself of meeting deadlines which stayed with him throughout his career. In 1970, he was appointed the Deputy Chief Engineer for the planning and design of Kolkata Metro, the first ever Metro in India.

In 1990, he was appointed the CMD of Konkan Railway, with a pre-condition that the government could not remove him from the position until the project was completed. Under his direction, the challenging and massive project of building a 760 km railway line through the rough Konkan terrain was completed within the stipulated time of seven years.

Dr. Shreedharan was a leader with impeccable integrity, with the ability to take bold and firm decisions. In addition he had an "aura" which comes from a person who is spiritually enlightened. His magnetic power and strength worked as a battery and a power house, which inspired and gave strength to the other executives. He had a good understanding of all the disciplines within DMRC and each person felt that he could go to him for guidance at all times.

Despite constantly being in the public eye, Dr. Shreedharan was known for his simple living and spiritual learning. He devoted three hours of his daily schedule to spiritual learning, meditation and yoga which helped him perform better, even in his 70s.

Professional Competency—DMRC Training Institute

Professional competency is one of the most valued qualities at DMRC. Having an in depth knowledge of the field and having enough experience to carry out the job, were two attributes expected from every individual employee at DMRC. Knowing the fact that India did not have prior experience and technical knowledge in putting together a MRTS, engineers were sent for specialized training programs, which included visits to international rail systems in Singapore, Hong Kong, Japan, Taipei, and so on., to increase their professional exposure. DMRC also appointed a foreign consultancy group called the General Consultants on a full time basis so that the engineers could absorb technical knowledge from these consultants directly.

The recruitment process at DMRC was transparent, with an All India competitive examination, which consisted of a written test, an interview and a detailed medical examination, on the patterns followed by the Union Public Service Commission (UPSC) and the Staff Selection Commission (SSC) of the GoI.

Since inception, DMRC has had a strong commitment to excellence in competency building in the field of rail based urban transportation systems. To meet the requirement, DMRC established its own Training Institute at Shastri Park Train depot in the year 2002. The Training Institute is ISO 9001:2015 accredited for design, development and delivery of training programs. It is equipped with state of the art training infrastructure and the most advanced simulators for training in the field of operations and maintenance. It is the only institute in the country which is equipped with all modern facilities to impart customized training on almost all aspects of operations and maintenance of rail based urban transportation systems. The Training Institute provides holistic training in terms of knowledge, skill and attitude along with physical, mental and spiritual health of the trainees.

It organizes executive training programs, management training programs, training programs for the DMRC staff and training programs for the clients as well. It also imparts training and consultancy to other Metro projects coming up in India.

The School's objective is "to harmonize and control training processes in order to enhance total productivity, develop competence for various job profiles and to provide training keeping abreast with changes in technology and continuously improving training processes."

Punctuality

The trains in Delhi Metro maintain a record of over 99 percent punctuality. Dr. Shreedharan believed that punctuality is important as ultimately the job of DMRC is to run trains, and if the DMRC team isn't punctual, we can't expect our trains to be punctual.

In the Delhi Metro, punctuality is sacrosanct as punctuality is a courtesy to the person with whom you are going to interact since his time is as precious and valuable as your own. Coming even a minute late is considered impolite and inappropriate. Arrival at the office at 9 a.m., which was the office timing, was considered absolutely essential, as Dr. Shreedharan believed that if you are late for office, you will be late in delivering the project. The same logic was stretched to the Metro train operations which led to Delhi Metro achieving a punctuality of over 99 percent. If a train was 60 seconds late, it was considered to have lost its punctuality.

To ensure punctuality, DMRC installed reverse clocks in every office and on site which recorded the number of days left for the completion of a particular section of the project. DMRC installed a master clock system to ensure that the same time was displayed at all of its offices, control rooms and stations to ensure that the whole organization worked with the same timeframe. The project team at DMRC followed a detailed process to ensure adherence to timelines. They would create an initial baseline diagram for themselves regarding the different contracts that they needed to finalize for each line, the proposed schedule and the materials and equipment to be procured. The team would analyze the layout for each corridor to anticipate possible hurdles (such as land that needed to be acquired as well as permissions and clearances that needed to be obtained), they then built key delivery dates into contracts and ensured that they were strictly adhered to.

An aspect of organizational structure that played a key role in maintaining timelines and adhering to deadlines was the quick decision making process. DMRC, as compared to other government agencies was created as a much leaner organization with only a handful of people responsible for decision making and a single point of clearance.

Though Dr. Shreedharan had the final say, there was a liberal delegation of powers at every level as DMRC believed in consensus. All the heads of departments and directors met in the MD's office on Monday mornings at 9:30 with no fixed or pre-decided agenda. The team would discuss the problems they were beset with and a decision would often be arrived at during the meeting itself, with documentation to support the decision, collated as a next step. The meeting also serve the dual purpose of bringing the various departments of DMRC up to speed with the work and issues of other departments. A variation of this Monday morning ritual was held on the first Monday of every month, where all middle level executives were also invited to the meeting with the top management to highlight the organization's priorities, targets and plans.

Integrity

Integrity doesn't stop at honesty or lack of corruption. It goes much beyond that. It is the quality of having good moral values. Anything that you do, you should do it in an upright fashion, in a transparent fashion.

—Dr. Shreedharan, Managing Director, DMRC

Integrity in DMRC is perceived as not only being honest but is also considered as a wider concept in which others perceive you to be honest. Dr. Shreedharan had built a "zero tolerance for corruption" attitude into DMRC's work ethic. If someone was found deviating from the path of honesty, or indulging in unfair practices, immediate action was taken and the person's association with DMRC was terminated. This institution of honesty, of knowing that each and every person's integrity was above board, also helped in speeding up the decision process. Dr. Shreedharan trusted his employees completely and attributed his ability to take decisions on the most complicated matters very quickly to this trust.

In DMRC, all employees are required to sign a code of ethics whose main contents are:

- DMRC employees should work with professionalism, honesty and integrity
- No employee shall indulge in giving or taking any illegal gratification, monetary or otherwise
- No employee should engage in lobbying or propose any honor or reward/award for himself
- No employee shall use his official position to further his personal interest
- No employee shall indulge in any trade or side business in his name

- No employee shall indulge in collection of any cause whatsoever without the management's prior approval
- No employee shall indulge in socially inappropriate behavior like indulging in bigamy/extra marital alliance, and so on
- Every employee shall assist and cooperate with the government to eliminate bribery, fraud or corruption
- Every employee shall spend every single rupee in the official discharge of his duty with diligence

All officers who are in the management cadre in DMRC are given a copy of the Bhagavad Gita, which is treated by DMRC as a management module and not as a spiritual or religious text as it explains how a person should manage himself so that he can function efficiently and give his best in every situation.

Social Responsibility and Accountability

In order to achieve its goal of being socially responsible, DMRC has taken several steps to ensure that onsite work causes minimal disruption to the lives of the residents of Delhi. Before it started work on any site, DMRC hired a traffic expert to study the roads surrounding the construction site and suggest minimally disruptive diversions. At times, DMRC had also resorted to acquiring land adjacent to the roads and widening them before starting the construction. The team discussed traffic and congestion issues with the police and took into account their suggestions, to reduce the bottlenecks and slowdowns as much as possible. DMRC engaged retired police officers who acted as a liaison between DMRC and the police department to keep the police from interfering and disrupting work at the project sites.

Before commencing construction in an area, DMRC organized community interaction sessions, in which the residents, politicians from that area, and even the press were invited. The briefing served the purpose of providing information about the work to be undertaken, and how it would affect their daily lives. People were encouraged to voice their opinions and wherever possible, DMRC adopted them if they were found to be feasible. The Chief Engineer of that area was introduced to the community as a go-to person in case of any problems. DMRC adopted the strategy of diverting utilities before the construction began, so that water lines, telephone lines and power cables remained intact as the work progressed.

DMRC used regular press releases regarding its future initiatives as a technique to keep the community informed and on board. DMRC had appointed a Chief Public Relations Officer (CPRO) to keep the media updated and informed about the ongoing projects and future initiatives.

DMRC, being a socially responsible organization, always accorded high priority to social causes. It conducted various awareness programs from time to time to educate its stakeholders. Some of the activities undertaken by DMRC are given as follows:

- For creating knowledge about HIV/AIDS/STI among labor engaged in the construction work, awareness programs were conducted from time to time. The medium used to spread awareness included banners, posters, street plays, songs, group discussions, counseling and magic shows.
- DMRC provided medical facilities and education services to its laborers and their children.
- A Children's Home, to accommodate 125 children, at Tis Hazari with five dormitories, two classrooms, a playground, an amphitheatre, a library and a mess was constructed by DMRC.
- A "Winter Age Home" was opened in Kalkaji near Govindpuri Metro Station, New Delhi. It is being run from November to March every year since 2011 in collaboration with the NGO "Help Age India" for the welfare of senior citizens.

DMRC installed rain water harvesting structures at elevated stations, viaducts, depots and staff colonies to provide an affordable means of accessing good quality water at the point of consumption. Currently DMRC has 553 rain water harvesting pits at 114 locations which have a total capacity of 11,203 cum. In the current FY 2017–2018, DMRC has planned to install five new RWH pits with a capacity of 50 cum.

From the very beginning of the project, DMRC took special care of the environment as Dr. Shreedharan believed it to be a very sensitive issue. In the DPR, an Environmental Impact Assessment (EIA) study for the project was conducted. DMRC had to cut around 30,000 trees in Phase-I and Phase-II, but it committed to the government that it would plant 10 trees for every tree cut as compensatory afforestation. It also transplanted a number of those trees which were eco-friendly and had good chances of survival after transplantation.

DMRC received the ISO 14001 and OHSAS 18001 certification for environmental protection and good environmental practices. It also became the first Railway System in the world to receive Carbon Credits for regenerative braking as DMRC trains save 33 percent of the energy lost during the braking process. DMRC helped in reduction in emission of harmful gases into the city's atmosphere and the United Nations Body administering the clean development mechanism (CDM) under the Kyoto Protocol has certified that DMRC has earned Carbon Credits worth INR 0.47 billion annually. Exhibit 3.1 depicts the network map of

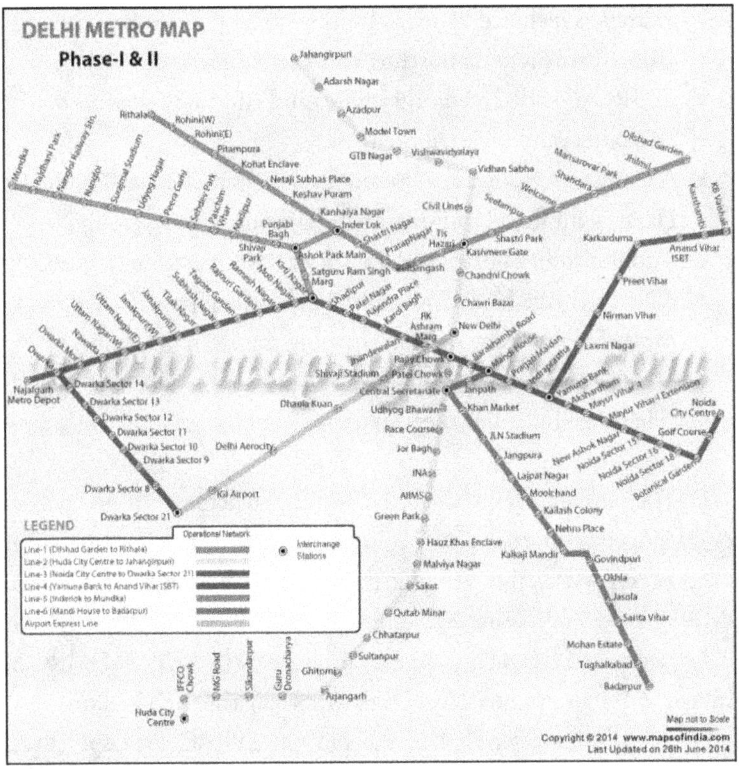

Exhibit 3.1 Delhi metro phase I and II network map

Source: DMRC.

Phase I and II. Exhibits 3.2 and 3.3 depict network maps of Phase III and IV, respectively. Exhibits 3.4 and 3.5 depict the accident sites at Lakshmi Nagar and Zamrudpur, respectively.

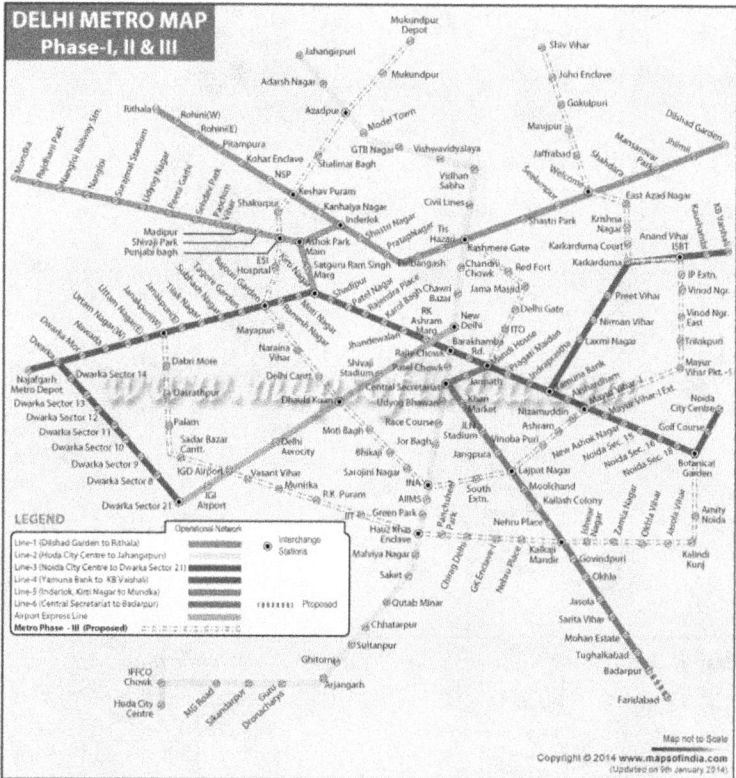

Exhibit 3.2 Delhi metro phase-III network map

Source: DMRC.

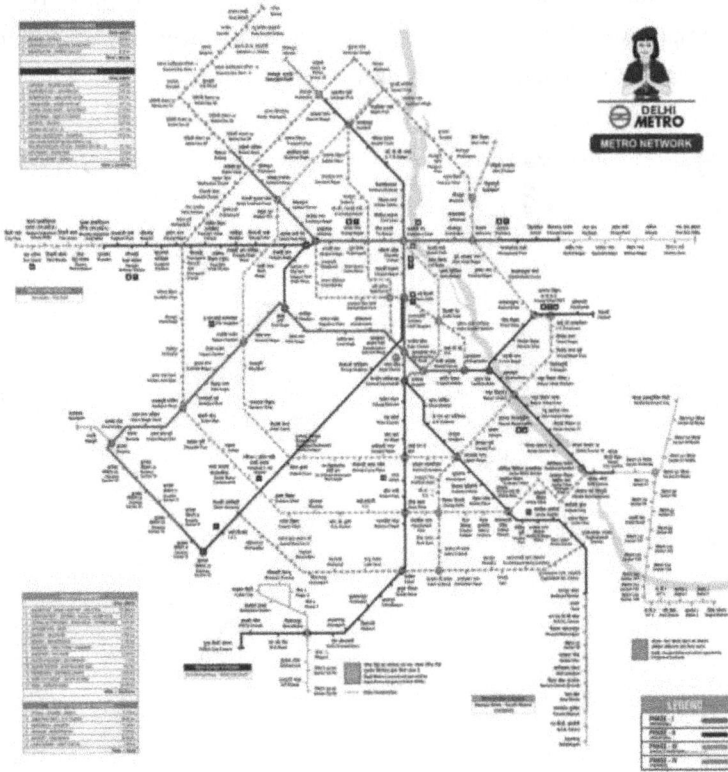

Exhibit 3.3 Delhi Metro Phase-IV proposed network map

Source: DMRC.

Exhibit 3.4 Accident site at Laxmi Nagar, October 19, 2008

Source: DMRC company documents.

Exhibit 3.5 Accident site at Zamradpur, July12, 2009

Source: DMRC Company documents.

References

Dayal, M.A. 2012. *25 Management Strategies for Delhi Metro*. Delhi Metro Rail Corporation Ltd.

Indian Institute for Human Settlements. 2015. *Urban Transport in India: Challenges and Recommendations*, 6–15. IIHS RF Paper on Urban Transport.

Narayan, V.G., and S. Chaturvedi. 2002. *A Case on Delhi Metro Rail Corporation*. Harvard Business School.

Ramachandran, M. 2012. *Metro Rail Projects in India: A Study in Project Planning*, 27–52. Oxford University Press.

CHAPTER 4

Pune Rainbow Bus Rapid Transit System

Background

Context

Pune is the eighth largest metropolis in the country and the second largest in the state of Maharashtra. It has been declared as a motor city due to proliferation of the automobile industry. Pimpri-Chinchwad and Pune are connected cities. Pune has systematically transformed from an agriculture based city into a vibrant industrial economy. It also emerges as one of the most important technological cities in India, as well as an important center of trade in the agricultural sector. As per the 2011 census, Pune city and the Pimpri-Chinchwad municipality cover about 450 and 181 square kilometers respectively, with a population of about 3.1 and 1.7 million in Pune and Pimpri-Chinchwad respectively (Rangarajan January 2010).

Transit System Before the Project

Traditionally recognized as a cycle city, Pune has turned out to be a metropolis of two wheelers. However, the city has moved toward using motorized means of transportation and this has led to an expansion in the municipal region along with a growth in population. The number of motorized vehicles rose to 2.7 million in 2001 to 2015 with the 10-year advancement level of 146 percent that resulted in an undesirable impression back at metropolis (Rangarajan January, 2010). According to RTO data of PimpriChinchwad, the number of private vehicles went up steeply which indicates a failure of public transport to meet the local demand. The modal share of municipal transportation was only four percent, pedestrian and bicycling constituted 17 percent, with the respect taken up by motorized private vehicles. Compared to the rest of the country, Pune has a smaller bus fleet size for every thousand individuals. The low share of public transport is possibly because of the proliferation of private vehicles combined with sluggish growth in the size of the bus fleet. High transit fares can rarely compete with a growing number of private fuel consumption modes, which are more reliable and more comfortable to move around in a big city and this is reflected in the modal stake as well. However, this trend can be reversed through service quality improvement, reliability of public transport and dis-incentivizing the use of private vehicles (Rangarajan January, 2010). Figure 4.1 illustrates carrying capacity of lanes at-level. Figure 4.2 illustrates that the capacity of lanes increase by 1.5 times, when lanes are raised at a level.

The BRTS Project

Motor vehicles produce high levels of pollution which is detrimental to public health. During peak hours, it can take up to three hours to cover a distance of five kilometer within Pune. Only a new transit system could counter all these issues and at the same time decongest the streets. Pune Municipal Corporation (PMC) devised a plan for BRTS with dedicated lanes and was successful in its implementation. This was expected to reduce road congestion and greenhouse gas emissions, despite a mixed traffic of motorized vehicles. Earlier, PimpriChinchwad Municipal

Figure 4.1 At level lanes

Source: PCMC presentation.

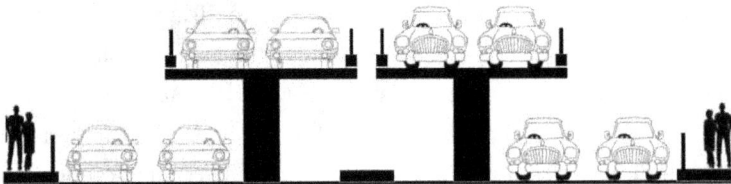

Figure 4.2 Raised lane: capacity increases by 1.5 times

Source: PCMC presentation.

Corporation (PCMC) had initiated the proposal for BRTS which four pilot projects with a total length of 45 kilometer. BRTS by PCMC was a part of the urban transit development strategy with the PMC, Pune Mahanagar Parivahan Mahamandal Ltd (PMPML) and Pune traffic police as the main stakeholders (Joshi 2010).

PMC and PCMC launched BRTS in an attempt to encourage multimodal transit along with a possible metro network. A number of countries have adopted BRT since it is a cost effective way to improve metro transit on a limited budget. Figure 4.3 illustrates the cross-section of the BRTS.

The advantages of BRT for the public are reduced travel time, better quality of and frequent service.

BRTS Plan

Pune, PimpriChinchwad municipalities jointly planned and implemented the BRTS with the financial backing of the JNNURM scheme, UNDP, SUTP and World Bank. These municipalities, with implementation support from ITDP, campaigns and outreach activities by IBI and CEE teams were able to significantly improve the pace of BRTS development (Parate and Shinde 2016).

Why BRTS Is the Right Solution

BRT is a long term project aimed at developing a well-organized and improved municipal transit conditions. BRT, with its higher load capacity, has gained the public's acceptance. The BRT proposed by the PMC was a significant phase in improving the transit planning in a city where commuter traffic was growing in a rapid manner. The share of public transit was tremendously low at 15 percent in 2012 and was projected to

Figure 4.3 BRTS Illustration

Source: PCMC presentation.

Table 4.1 Comparison of BRT with alternate travel modes

Sr. No.	Parameters	BRT	LRT/mono rail/trams	Metro
1	Construction cost per kilometer	Rs. 15–20 Cr	Rs 100–120 Cr	Rs. 160–180 Cr
2	Cost of locomotive	Non AC—Rs. 0.3 Cr AC—Rs. 0.8–1 Cr	Rs. 8–10 Cr	Rs. 10–12 Cr
3	Accessibility	12%	At grade or overhead	Underground or overhead
4	Route modification	4%	Fixed	Fixed

Source: PimpriChinchwad Municipal Corporation.

come down to 10 percent in 2031 if no action was taken. Once BRT was implemented, the share of public transport was expected to increase to 60 percent by 2031. (PMC PCMC 2013). The existing and projected modal shares as a percentage are presented in Figure 4.4. Table 4.1 compares BRT features with other travel modes. Table 4.2 presents the significant features of modern urban transport modes. Figure 4.5 is an actual representation of the Pune BRTS.

Pune Profile

Demographic Trends

Population

Pune has a population of nearly 3.11 million as per the 2011 Census, which is six times that in 1951, mainly driven by the commercial development under PMC. PCMC has a population of 1.35 million as of 2011 census, an increase of 150 percent over 1,990 figures (Urban Mass Transit Company Limited November 2012). Figure 4.6 illustrates the population growth in Pune over the years. The projected decadal population growth is presented in Table 4.3 and illustrated in Figure 4.7.

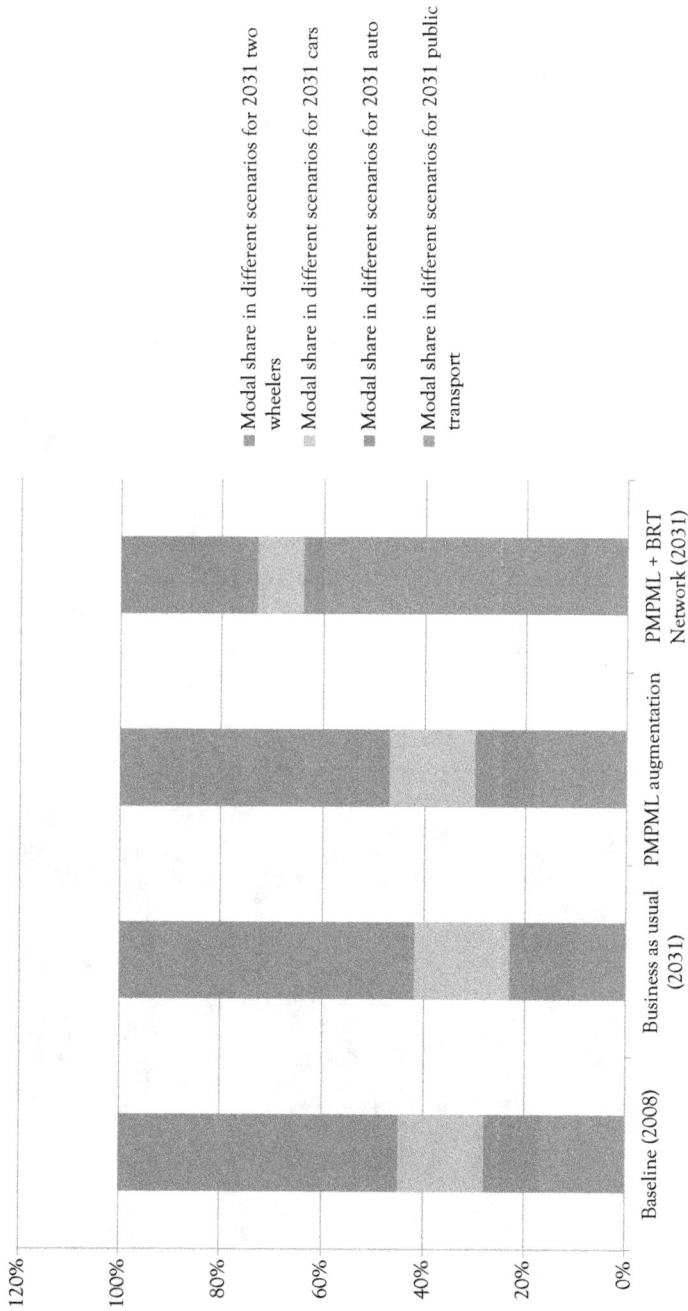

Figure 4.4 Paybacks of BRT

Source: Comprehensive mobility plan, Pune (2008).

Table 4.2 Strategic features of high quality transit system

	BRT	Metro	LRT	Monorail
Dedicated row	Yes	Yes	Yes	Yes
Safe, easy level boarding-alighting	Yes	Yes	Yes	Yes
Automatic fare collection	Yes	Yes	Yes	Yes
Real—time passenger information	Yes	Yes	Yes	Yes
High quality service can attract users from personal vehicles	Yes	Yes	Yes	Yes
Quick and easy access to stations	Yes	No	Yes/No	No
Capacity over >20,000 pphpd	Yes	Yes	No	No
Multiple routers per corridor	Yes	No	No	No
Express services	Yes	No	No	No
Affordability for customers and the city	Yes	No	No	No

Source: PCMC presentation.

Figure 4.5 BRT corridors

Source PCMC presentation.

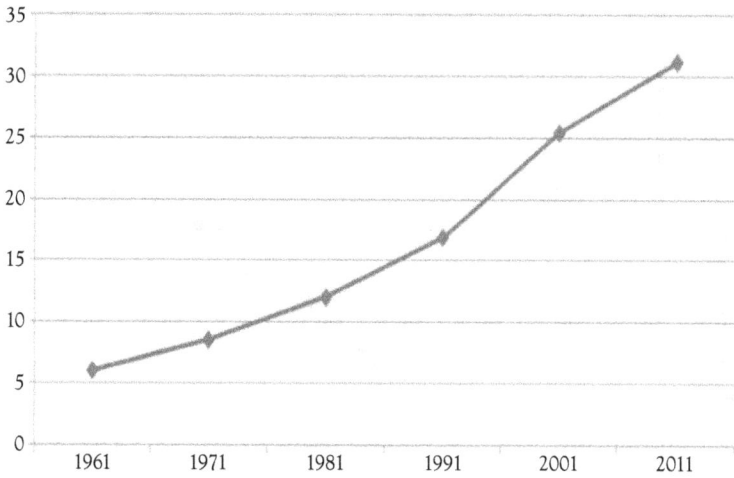

Figure 4.6 Population growth in Pune (in lakhs)

Source: Census 2011.

Table 4.3 Decadal population growth rate in Pune

Census years	Population	Decadal change	Decadal growth rate (%)
1991	5,20,639	2,68,870	106.79
2001	10,06,417	4,85,778	93.3
2011	15,07, 243	5,00,826	49.76
2021	21,50,317	6,43,074	42.67
2031	29,07,757	7,57,440	35.22

Population Progress Level

Figure 4.8 depicts the rate of population change in the PMC area; a steady increase is observed from 1961 to 1971 and then there is a flat growth rate for two decades. There is a steep increase from 1991 to 2001, predominantly due to the economic growth driven by IT enabled services (ITES) industries in PMC. The decline from 50 percent to 22 percent of population growth from 2001 to 2011 is due to development of engineering zone in PCMC and therefore the shifting of Pune population to the

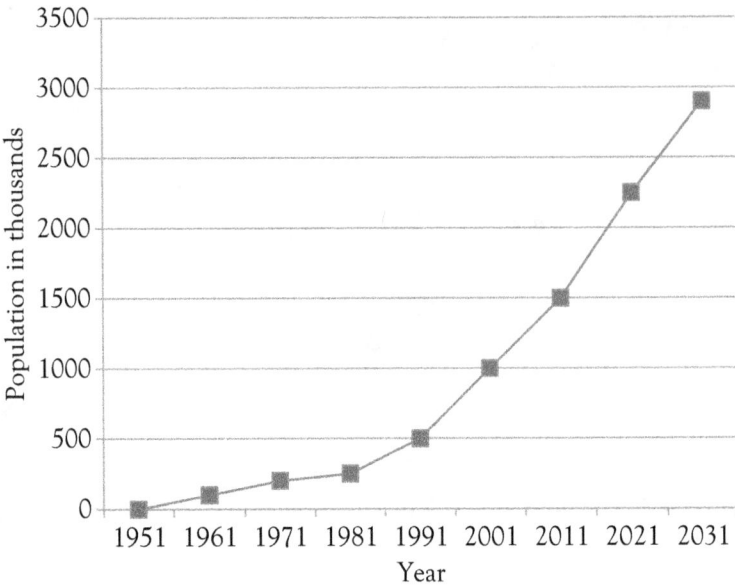

Figure 4.7 Projected population growth in PCMC

Source: Urban Mass Transit Company Limited, New Delhi (November 2012).

PCMC region. (PMC, Detailed Project Report for Financial Assistance under MoUD Scheme for Purchase of Buses).

Population Density

The density of population in Pune rose from 462 individuals/square kilometer in 2001 to 603 individuals per square kilometer in 2011 (Census 2011).

Gender Ratio

The gender ratio in Pune as per the 2001 and 2011 census was 916 and 945 women per thousand men correspondingly (PMC, Detailed Project Report for Financial Assistance under MoUD Scheme for Purchase of Buses).

Urban Economy

Pune's Gross Domestic Product (GDP) in 2010 was USD 23 billion, with a growth of 15 percent year on year, and its per capita income grew

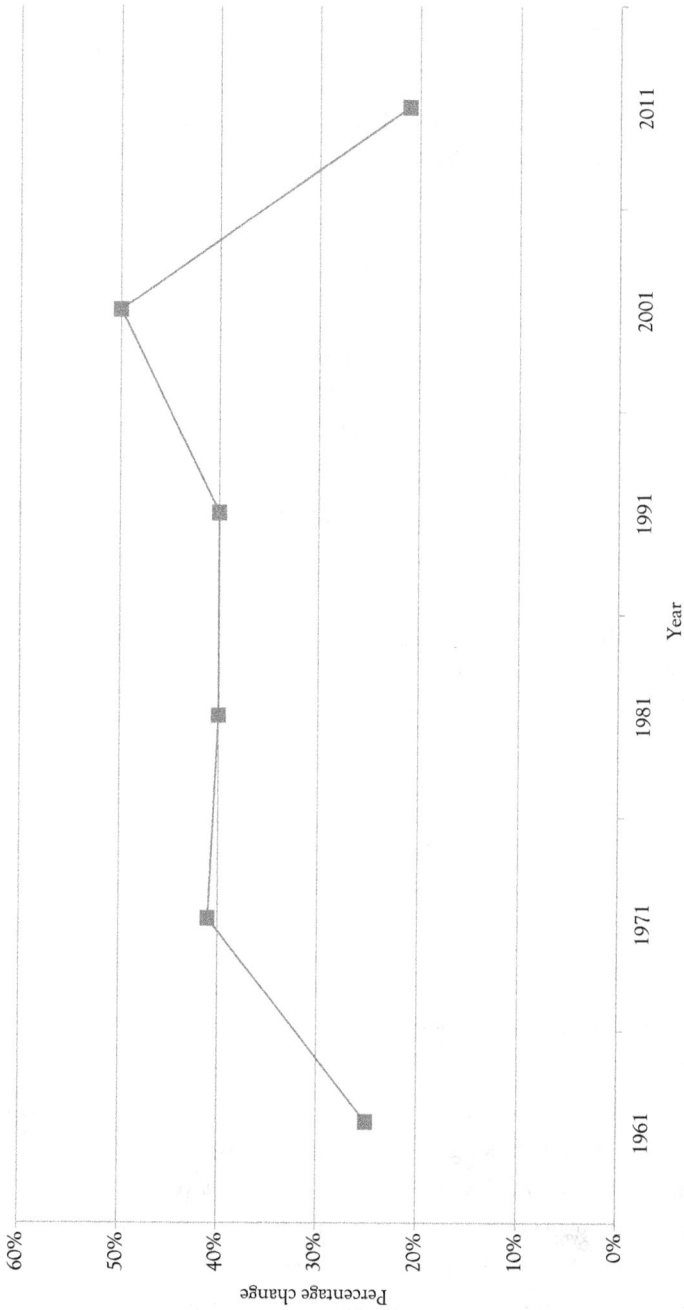

Figure 4.8 Rate of Population change in Pune

Source: Census 2011.

at six percent for the same period. Figure 4.9 shows that Pune is the sixth richest metropolis in the country; mainly it is due to the presence of the engineering and training sectors (PMC, Detailed Project Report for Financial Assistance under MoUD Scheme for Purchase of Buses).

The per capita revenue of the populace by way of ESR information in 2011 was 60thousand, which is twice that in 2004. The labor partaking level as of 2001 census was 34 percent, which was greater thru two percent in contrast with that in 1991 (PMC, Detailed Project Report for Financial Assistance under MoUD Scheme for Purchase of Buses).

Land Use

In 2001, the PMC was spread over 138.36 square kilometers. In 1966, PMC implemented its first 10 year development plan whose focus was urban development. This plan was revised to a 20 year plan in 1987. Tables 4.4 and 4.5 present the terrestrial land usage in PMC in PCMC respectively. Figure 4.10 illustrates the terrestrial distribution in PMC.

In line with the DP 1987, 43 percent of the area was for housing, 16 percent for public utilities, around 30 percent for commercial purposes, with the rest being taken up by the unorganized sector. (Urban Mass Transit Company Limited November 2012).

Existing Road Networks

Services

Street Networks, Pune

Overcrowded streets in the central zone along with the topographical division of the metropolis which aimed at preserving historical landmarks lead to complex inter-linkages across sectors. The municipal buses steered clear of these sectors, making access to public transport difficult. As per the Center for Training Transportation Professionals (CTTP) in 2001, 4.5 percent of the terrestrial space in the metropolis region was for road construction; only 25 percent of the city roads had a width 24 meter or more (PMC, Detailed Project Report for Financial Assistance under MoUD Scheme for Purchase of Buses).

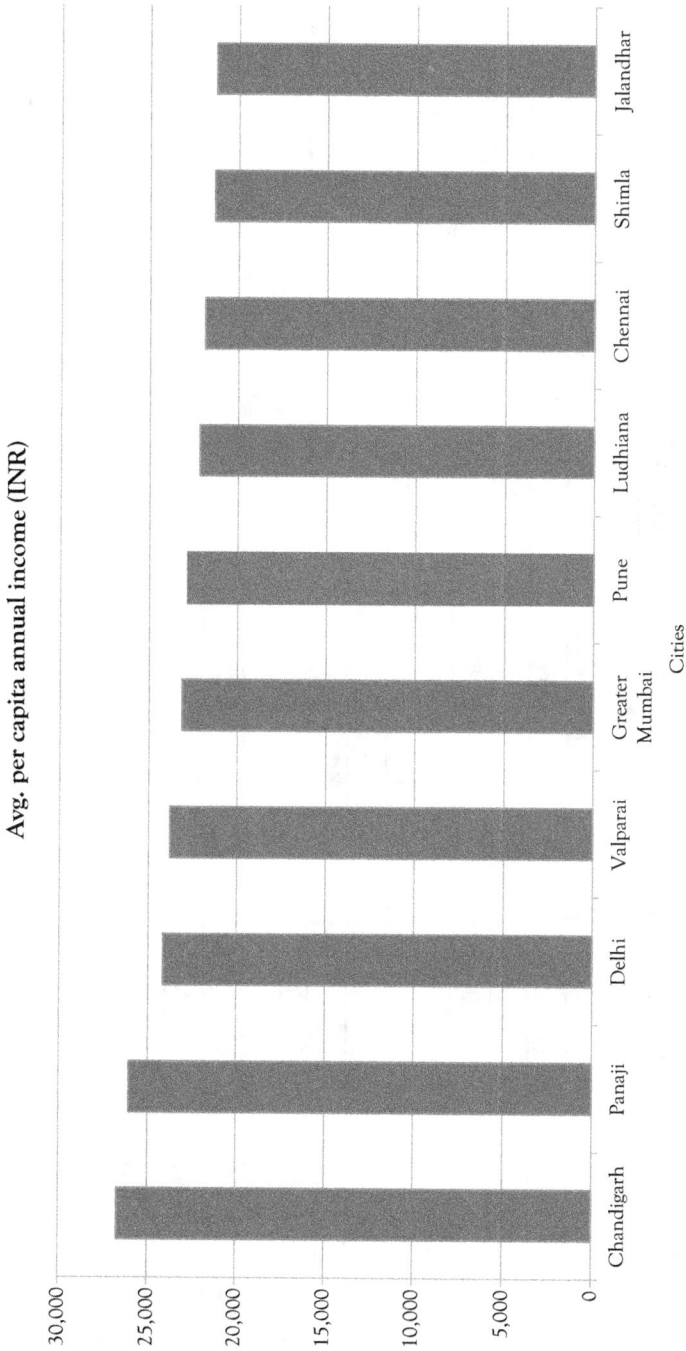

Figure 4.9 Bar chart depicting the richest metropolises in India

Source: Karve Institute of Social Service Report, 2008–2009.

Table 4.4 *Terrestrial usage outline, PMC*

Land use category	1987 DP Square kilometer	2001 DP Square kilometer	Total Square kilometer	1987 DP %	2001 DP %	Total %
Residential	50.58	53.16	103.74	36.56	50.35	42.53
Commercial	2.35	1.57	3.92	1.7	1.49	1.61
Industrial	7.26	2.62	9.88	5.25	2.48	4.05
Public and semi-public	15.22	1.45	16.67	11	1.37	6.83
Public utilities	1.38	....	1.38	1	....	0.57
Transport	22	9.81	31.81	15.9	9.29	13.04
Reserved forest and agriculture	2.35	26.7	29.05	1.7	25.29	11.91
Water bodies	12.04	2.48	14.52	8.7	2.35	5.95
Hills and hill slopes	12.45	....	12.45	9	....	5.1
Recreational	12.73	7.79	20.52	9.2	7.38	8.41
Total	138.36	105.58	243.94	100	100	100

Source: Bus funding DPR under MoUD scheme, Pune

Table 4.5 *Terrestrial usage outline, PCMC*

Sl No.	Head	Existing			Proposed in draft DP		
		Area (square kilometer)	Area developed (%)	Total area (%)	Area (square kilometer)	Area developed (%)	Total area (%)
1	Residential	22.6	80.84	26.34	17.28	67.25	55.94
2	Commercial	0.19	9.70	0.23	2.68	3.81	3.17
3	Industrial	1.18	5.37	1.75	3.22	4.58	3.81
4	Public utilities	0.39	1.43	0.47	0.97	1.37	1.14
5	Public and semi public	0.82	2.99	0.97	2.66	3.78	3.15
6	Transportation/circulation	2.38	8.63	2.81	10.94	15.57	12.95
7	Open spaces recreation	0.01	0.05	0.01	2.56	3.64	3.03
8	Water bodies	0.95		1.13	1.33		1.57
9	Quarry	2.46		2.91			0.00
10	Barren/vacant lands	20.29		24.00			0.00
11	Agriculture and reserve forest	33.27		39.37	12.89		15.25
	Sub—Total (development area)	27.54	100.00	32.59	70.29	109.86	83.18
	Sub—Total (un-development area)	56.97		67.41	14.22		16.82
	Total	84.51			84.51		

Source: Urban Mass Transit Company Limited, New Delhi (November 2012)

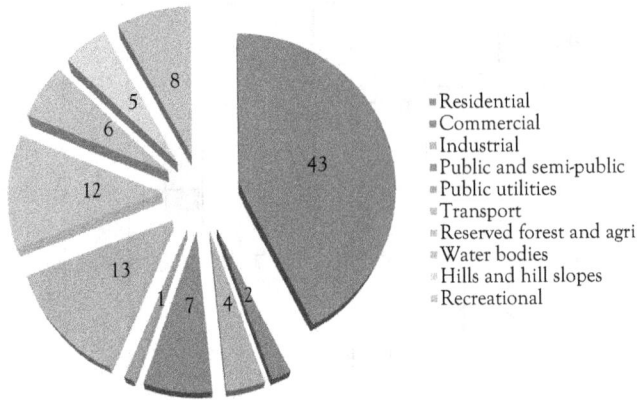

Legend:
- Residential
- Commercial
- Industrial
- Public and semi-public
- Public utilities
- Transport
- Reserved forest and agri
- Water bodies
- Hills and hill slopes
- Recreational

Figure 4.10 *Proportion of terrestrial usage, PMC*

Source: Bus funding DPR under MoUD scheme, Pune.

Road Networks, PimpriChinchwad

Most of the PCMC zone has a well-connected network of streets linking the chief commuter traffic lanes and feeder routes. There were a number of narrow streets in the former PCMC zone in contrast to the first-hand zone of the northern as well as western regions. Most roads had few encroachments unlike the sub arterial roads. The length of the road network was 757 kilometer, of which 667 kilometer was built as Modern Bitumen roads, 4.95 kilometer had a reinforced concrete and 85 kilometer were built as Water Bound Macadam (WBM). The PCMC maintained the national and state highways; the share of RoW in PCMC is given in the Table 4.6 (Urban Mass Transit Company Limited November 2012).

Pedestrian and NMV Facilities

Factually, Pune is the cycle metropolis of the country but travelling by bicycle has declined due to the greater than before usage of motorized vehicles. The modal stake of bicycling in 2001 was 11 percent. This might due to the lack of dedicated lanes for bicycles which makes it dangerous to move alongside motorized traffic. Street vendors invading the roadways have further narrowed the available road width, forcing pedestrians to walk on the road, thus creating unsafe conditions. As per the study

Table 4.6 *Percentage of street length by way of RoW*

RoW (meter)	% Road length in PCMC
Upto 10	4.5%
10 to 15	18.5%
15 to 20	34.0%
20 to 30	28.5%
30 to 40	7.0%
40 to 60	5.7%
above 60	2.0%
Total	100%

Source: Urban Mass Transit Company Limited, New Delhi (November 2012)

conducted, nearly half of the streets had no sidewalks on either side (PMC, Detailed Project Report for Financial Assistance under MoUD Scheme for Purchase of Buses).

Traffic Management

There were no structured street-parking services in most of the areas due to lack of land space. Later PMC allocated 9,000 slots for motorized vehicle parking near 14 sites. Lack of parking spaces and organized parking facilities resulted in messy and disorganized parking in most commercial areas. One of the key reasons for the narrow road widths was automobiles parked on the sides. Narrow roads and a large number of motorized vehicles resulted in road congestion. The typical speed was 20 kilometer per hour during peak periods through clogged traffic in numerous roads (PMC, Detailed Project Report for Financial Assistance under MoUD Scheme for Purchase of Buses).

Road Safety

Over the past few years, road related accidents and fatalities had increased. As per RTO records of 2001, based on data collected on a monthly basis from July 2006 to June 2007, majority of the accidents were due to PMT buses and not because of private buses. The comparative data of number of persons in every 10,000 passengers affected by road accidents involving Private and PMT buses is plotted in Figure 4.11. (PMC, Detailed Project Report for Financial Assistance under MoUD Scheme for Purchase of Buses).

Figure 4.12 displays the accident related data from 2001 to 2010. The number of fatalities was the highest at 458 in 2007, with 634 commuters grievously injured. Post the BRTS implementation and operation in 2007, the number of accidents and fatalities has been continuously declining. (PMC, Detailed Project Report for Financial Assistance under MoUD Scheme for Purchase of Buses).

Vehicle Composition

As per RTO, the total number of automobiles had increased by 10 percent annually with the number of additional vehicles in 2007 to 2010 being more than 1.34 lakh. An increasing population combined with higher GDP resulted in an increased travel demand. However, this growth led to poor air quality and further road crowding. A similar situation is seen in PCMC as well with a vehicle growth of more than 13 percent, (illustrated in Figure 4.13) most of which are two-wheelers followed by four wheelers (Urban Mass Transit Company Limited November 2012).

The mobility demand has increased due to industrialization. Traffic in the city of Pune is characterized by the presence of both inter and intra city traffic. Earlier, people used to cycle, now, they have moved to motorized automobiles (RTO 2012).

Figure 4.14 illustrates the proportion of automobiles in 2011 to 2012. As per RTO, as many as 775 automobiles are being registered each day, which led to increased traffic and congestion. Poor municipal transport facilities led to people choosing personal motorized vehicles.

Features of Traffic Flow on the Streets

Approach Toward Better Mobility, Pune

People generally preferred to commute on foot or by cycle, despite the fact that two wheelers accounted for 71 percent of the total vehicles in the city. Only two percent used municipal buses (PMC, Detailed Project

Private PMT buses

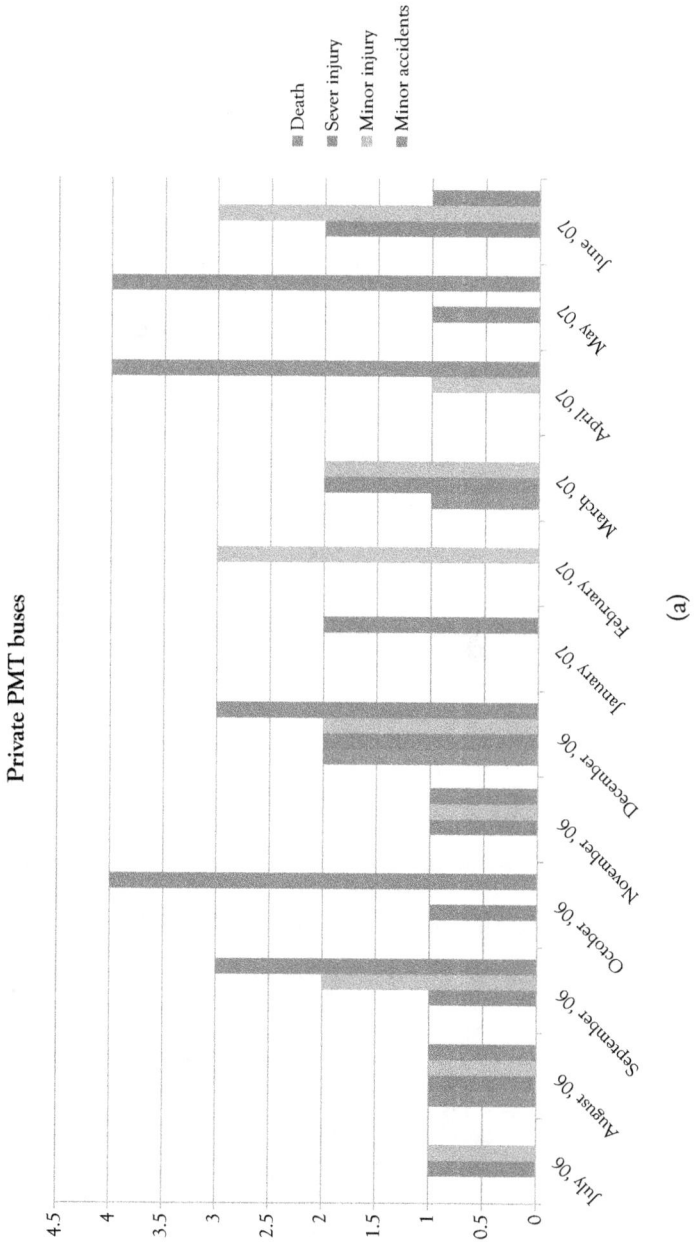

Legend: Death, Sever injury, Minor injury, Minor accidents

(a)

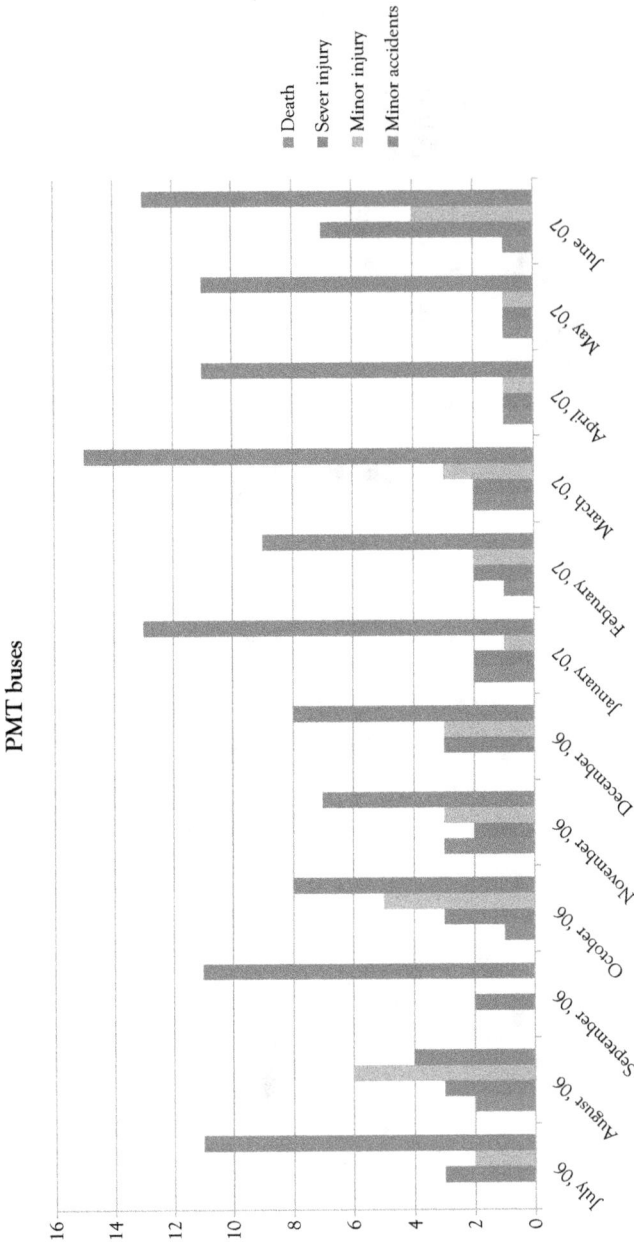

Figure 4.11 *Comparative data of accidents of private and PMT buses in Pune*

Source: PMT, Swargate Depot, Pune.

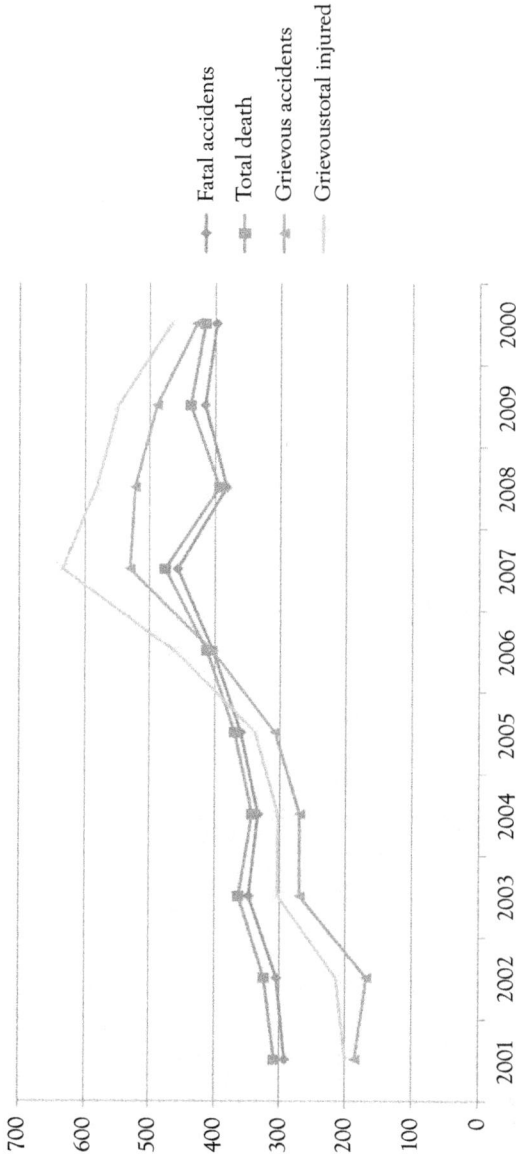

Figure 4.12 **Fatal and grievous accidents in Pune over 10 years**

Source: Accidents department, traffic police, PCMC.

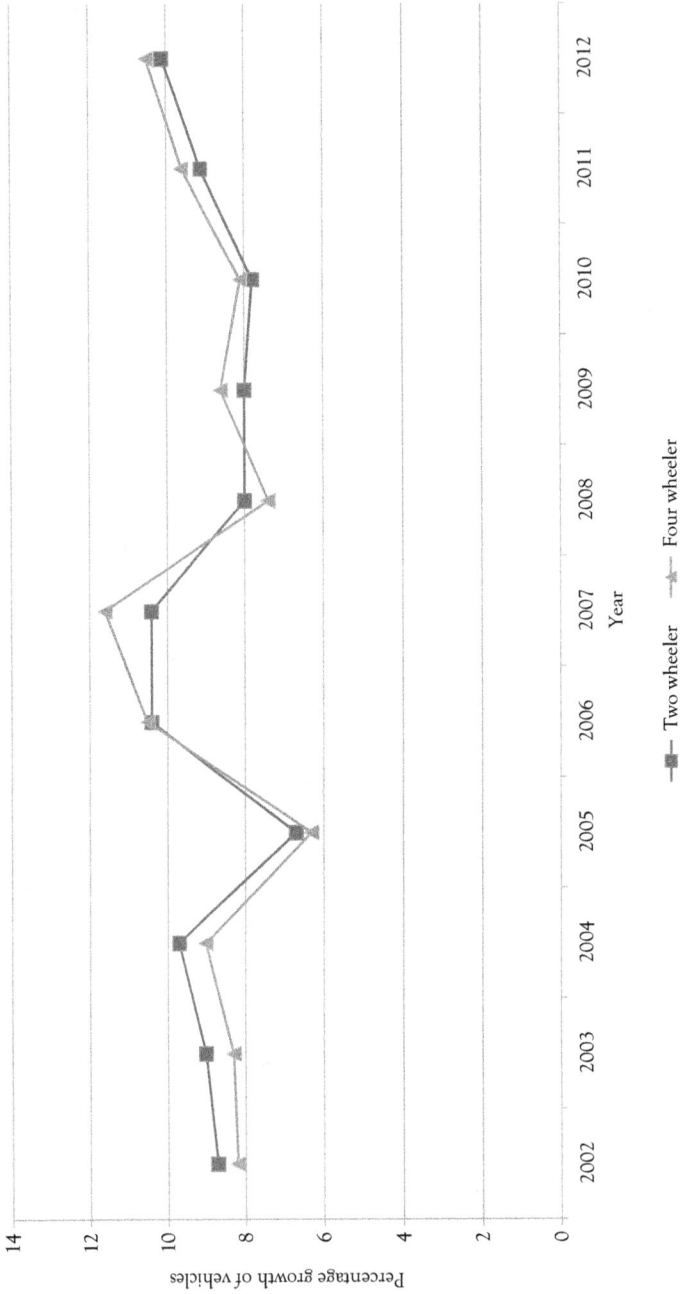

Figure 4.13 Vehicle progressions 2001–2012, Pune

Source: Regional Transport Office, Pune, 2012.

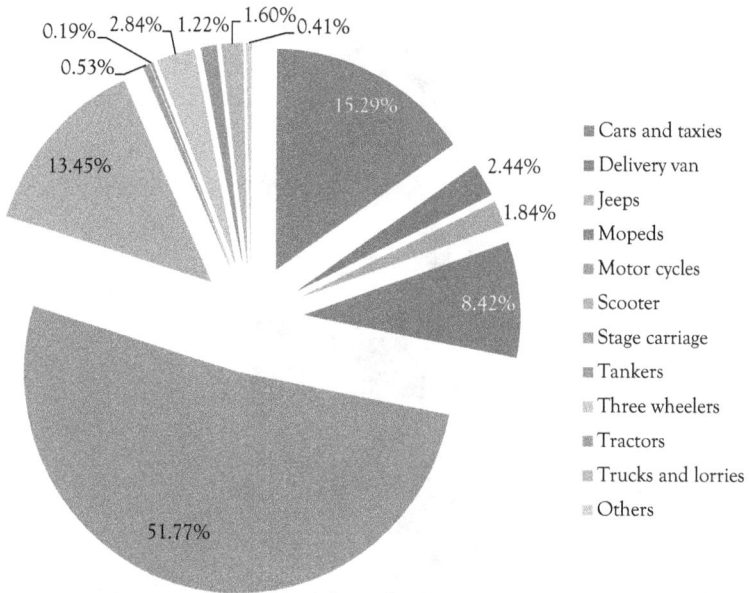

Figure 4.14 Vehicle composition, 2011–2012, Pune

Source: Regional transport office, Pune, 2012.

Report for Financial Assistance under MoUD Scheme for Purchase of Buses), as illustrated in Figure 4.15

Approach Toward Sensible Mobility, PimpriChinchwad

Most people worked in industries in the PCMC zone. As a result, they had to undertake frequent trips between the paired metropolises. While most commuters preferred personal motorized vehicles in PCMC, an interesting fact reported by RITES was pedestrians and cycling constituted 76 percent of the total modal share whereas municipal transit represented only 11 percent (Urban Mass Transit Company Limited November 2012). The modal share in PimpriChinchwad is tabulated in Table 4.7.

Transit Characteristics

The congestion increased in the past few years with the main reason being the substantial escalation of personal motorized means of transportation

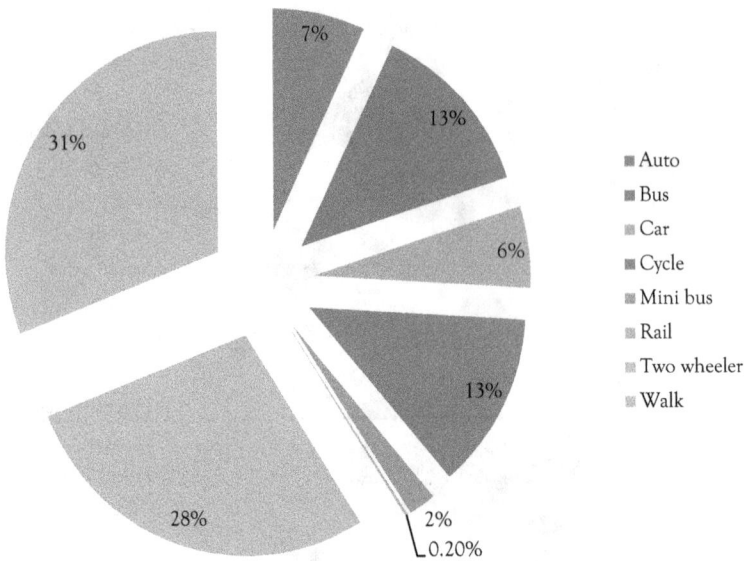

Figure 4.15 Modal share of commuting in Pune

Source: Bus funding DPR under MoUD scheme–Pune.

Table 4.7 Modal share of commuting in PimpriChinchwad

Sr. No.	Modes	% of total trips
1	Walk	58.39
2	Two wheelers	10.49
3	Cycle	18.03
4	Bus	10.72
5	Auto	1.67
6	Cars	0.44
7	Rail	0.35
Total		100

Source: RITES (1998).

along with the deficiency of municipal transit alternatives. Typically, there were merely 37 buses for every one lakh individuals falling short of 55 as a point of reference. This meant a share of merely 20 percent in public transit compared to an ideal 50 percent (PMC, Detailed Project Report for

Financial Assistance under MoUD Scheme for Purchase of Buses). The occupation prospects were increasing at the periphery of the metropolis; therefore, the everyday commuting distance was around 10 kilometers. Even with trips that were less than 5 kilometers, commuting was hard for that on foot or on bicycles,

Municipal Transit System

PMPML looks after the municipal transit system of the metropolis. PMC and PCMC operated on 370 routes with a fleet size of 1,800 buses (PMC, Detailed Project Report for Financial Assistance under MoUD Scheme for Purchase of Buses).

Intermediate Transit

The chief modes of intermediate transportation services were autos, which drove along the same roads as buses and offered better commuting in narrow streets. This affected municipal transit adversely resulting in fewer commuters. Autos are useful in areas that are not well connected and they are also cheaper than other modes (PMC, Detailed Project Report for Financial Assistance under MoUD Scheme for Purchase of Buses).

Municipal Transit Commuters

Table 4.8 provides data about the modal share of commuters per day in Pune city during 2008 to 2012 and commuter distribution is presented in Table 4.9.

Operational Details of PMPML and PCMT

Table 4.10 depicts the operational details of PMPML and PCMT during 2000 to 2008.

The bus fleet size did not change much in spite of the increasing demand. As a result, municipal buses were forced to operate along many different routes on a given day. This led to delays for commuters. (Urban Mass Transit Company Limited November 2012).

Table 4.8 Modal share, Pune

Type of mode	Number of fleet				Average daily ridership			
	2008–2009	2009–2010	2010–2011	2011–2012	2008–2009	2009–2010	2010–2011	2011–2012
City bus system	1,511	1,620	1,565	1,634	971,250	1,172,424	1,236,176	1,177,164

Source: Bus funding DPR under MoUD scheme, Pune.

Table 4.9 Commuters data, PCMT

Year	No. of buses	Buses on road	No of passenger/day
1999–2000	215	130	55,674
2000–2001	232	142	60,989
2001–2002	232	121	54,684
2002–2003	232	111	59,192
2003–2004	187	109	75,627
2004–2005	212	123	83,192

Source: Urban Mass Transit Company Limited, New Delhi (November 2012).

BRTS Design

Introduction

In 2006, the MoUD framed the NUTP with guiding principles to improve the existing transit schemes. In line with these objectives, PMC embarked on a number of development schemes such as a comprehensive mobility strategy, metro project and BRTS. A design document was developed with appropriate policy features, conceptualization of maintenance and progress monitoring (Pune Municipal Corporation 2016).

Topology of Roads

Category of Streets Planned

Basis: Street classification strategies considered providing road traffic features that would ensure RoW accommodating diverse utilities, commuter movement, and existing infrastructure.

Mobility Corridors

The comprehensive mobility plans were developed by analyzing commuter traffic and connectivity, which were responsible for almost 80 percent of the road traffic flow. The implementation plan had to ensure that minimal disturbance was caused to the commuter and to the traffic.

Table 4.10 Operational details of PCMT, PMPML

No	Parameter	Units	2000–2001	2001–2002	2002–2003	2003–2004	2004–2005	2005–2006	2006–2007	2007–2008
1	Fleet strength	(Nos.)	232	232	232	212	262	288	1,214	1,287
2	Effective kilometers	(Million)	15	11	11	11	12	14	7	7
3	Kilometers/bus/day	(Kilometers)	284	259	280	281	266	264	231	234
4	Fleet utilization	(%)	61	52	48	55	58	59	74	75
5	Occupancy ratio	(%)	34	37	45	50	53	52	75	76
6	Bus staff ratio	(Nos.)	14	16	17	14	15	16	10	9
7	Accidents/million kilometer	(Nos.)	8	5	6	5	6	5	4.1	3.9
8	Breakdown/10,000 kilometer	(INR)	8	10	11	13	16	14	1.52	0.68

Source: Urban Mass Transit Company Limited, New Delhi (November 2012).

Passages for NMT and pedestrian pathways were also incorporated in the design (Pune Municipal Corporation 2016).

Feeder Routes

Feeder routes provide the end mile connectivity between the major corridors and customer destinations. Figure 4.16 illustrates street topology in Pune and Figure 4.17 illustrates the lane features.

Components of the Road

Walkways

The walkways are dedicated passages for pedestrians, which provide safe access between parking spaces and the BRT corridors. As per global policies on RoW and depending on the type of roads, a space of two meter width is necessary for unhindered pedestrian movement (Pune Municipal Corporation 2016).

Figure 4.16 Map of street typology, Pune

Source: Urban Street Design Guidelines, Pune (July 2016).

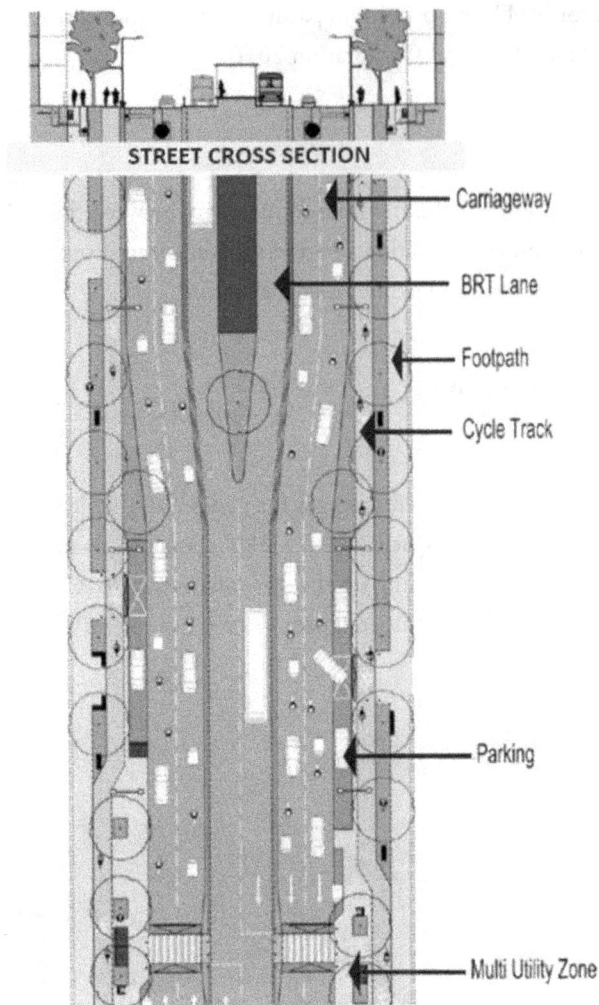

STREET CROSS SECTION

- Carriageway
- BRT Lane
- Footpath
- Cycle Track
- Parking
- Multi Utility Zone

Figure 4.17 Design outline demonstrating lane features

Source: Urban Street Design Guidelines, Pune (July 2016).

It is also necessary that pedestrian passages should be slightly above the road level with a 150 millimeter curb separation (Pune Municipal Corporation 2016). A smooth ramp for inward and outward movement to the parking space and for road access for differently-abled people was included as part of the design. However, autos and two wheelers used such pedestrian passages for parking, which made pedestrian movement unsafe.

Bicycle Lanes

Dedicated bicycle lanes were meant to restrict reckless motorized vehicles. A two meter wide lane was required for movement in one direction while a three meter wide lane was needed for bi-directional movement. The bicycle lanes should be smoothened through the application of surface treatments. Bicycle lanes should have signage boards and signals at intersections, should be well lit, and should have lanes markers at the beginning and end of the track to prohibit the entry of vehicles into this lane (Pune Municipal Corporation 2016).

Bus Stops

Bus stops are an important component of the BRTS since their location impacts other vehicular movements. Underground passages, if required, must be well planned to accommodate the anticipated increase in pedestrian movement as well as existing bus stops.

The bus stops must be close to intersections and no parking should be allowed at a 50 meter distance from the bus stops. These stops must be easy to get to from pedestrian overpasses. There should be no walkways; bicycle and service lanes anywhere near the BRTS. The bus stop should be well lit at night (Pune Municipal Corporation 2016).

Dedicated Lanes for BRT Buses

Dedicated bus lanes are a unique feature of the BRTS, which significantly transforms mobility at a moderate investment.

Design References of BRT Lanes

These dedicated lanes for BRT buses enable rapid movement along the roads by minimizing interruptions from other vehicular movements. Fewer buses can satisfy the commuter requirements, thus making the BRT and low cost means of transport. The BRT lanes are dedicated lanes of 7 meter width on 30 meter wide roads, with medians separating them from other vehicular movements (Pune Municipal Corporation 2016). An illustration is presented in Figure 4.18.

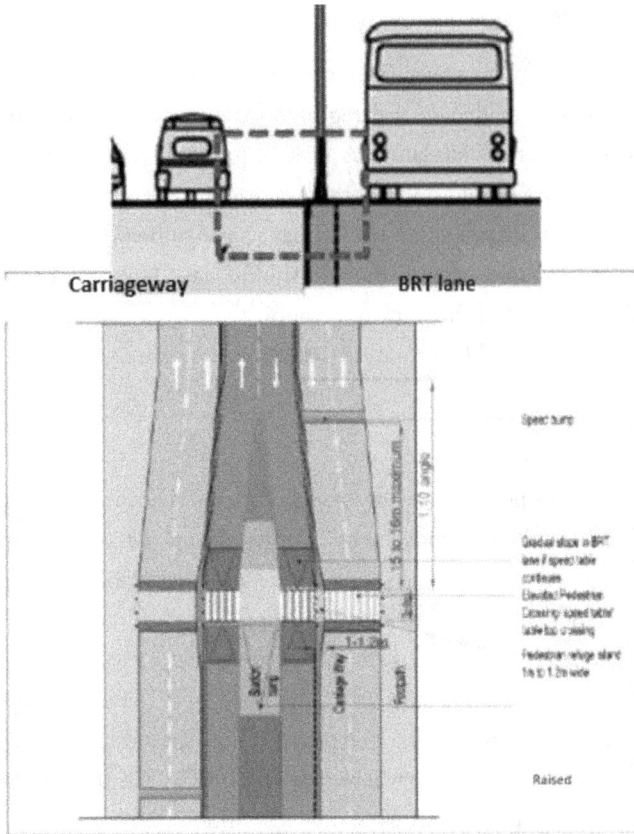

Figure 4.18 Cross section of proposed plan

Source: (Pune Municipal Corporation 2016).

Case 1: Over the Existing Prevailing Median

The design recommended steady gradient to facilitate pedestrian movements.

Case 2: BRT Lane on an Additional Street Along Existing Lane

The design recommendation was to construct the BRT at a 150 millimeter elevation from the existing motorized lanes, to make the stations accessible to pedestrians (Pune Municipal Corporation 2016).

Carriageway

The BRT lanes had well-demarcated path markings as well as barricades to ensure RoW for BRT and to prevent unauthorized parking.

The width of the road must be uniform over the entire length of the road except at the intersections, where the grading would (Pune Municipal Corporation 2016).

Shoulders

The shoulder provides appropriate height to ensure that the surface water from the roadway can move to the side drains; the shoulder compensates for the lack of availability of a footpath.

NMT was also allocated dedicated space so that the distance between the normal vehicular traffic and the BRT allowed for smooth movement of traffic (Pune Municipal Corporation 2016). Figure 4.19 illustrates a road design for alleviating congestions.

Street Parking

Generally, people park their motorized vehicles on the street, so the municipal authorities depending on the RoW, have created designated parking spaces to tackle this problem. Restricted parking space of 50 meter at critical positions and curbs, clear the pathways for uninterrupted pedestrian movement (Pune Municipal Corporation 2016).

Curb and Slope Ramp

Curb ramps are essential structures for smooth mobility of wheelchair users provided the level difference is less than 150 millimeter, when it

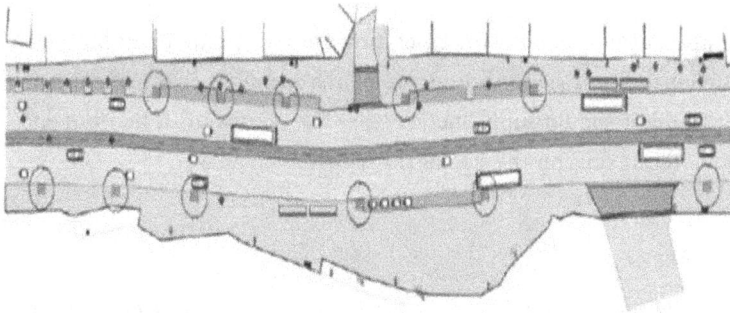

Figure 4.19 Design to alleviate bottlenecks

Source: (Pune Municipal Corporation 2016).

is more than 150 millimeter, the ramp should be sloping, and for even greater level differences, options such as elevators were used (Pune Municipal Corporation 2016).

Security Features

Pedestrian Overpass

Provision of crossings is essential next to all intersections for safe passage across the motorized lanes. There should be a short unhindered path across the road to make pedestrian crossing easy and safe. Depending on the number of commuters and traffic, overpasses of three meter width have been built. Zebra crossings are necessary at all transit intersections and should be painted in reflective white (Pune Municipal Corporation 2016).

Central Median Markers

The railings should be made of sturdy material and should be aesthetic enough to improve the appearance of the street. They should be 1.1 meter high so that people cannot climb over them (Pune Municipal Corporation 2016). Markers may have different shapes and designs, but should not come in the way of pedestrians or cyclists. They should be placed close to intersections to avert motorized vehicles from the BRT corridors. The combination of markers and guardrails prevents vehicles from moving on to the footpaths near the intersections.

Speed Breakers

Bumps and humps were the chief categories of speed circuit breakers on municipal motorways. Appropriate marks and signs that make them visible at night should supplement them. The bumps must be from end to end without slots on the side of the road.

Lighting

BRT corridors, medians, pedestrian movements to and from the BRT stops should be well lit. The lighting should be synchronous with the signs and bulletin boards (Pune Municipal Corporation 2016).

Road Signs and Marks

The signs must be clearly visible and should be placed on the left side of the road.

Traffic Signals and Indicators at Intersections

Traffic signals at intersections permit right of way to ensure smooth and safe travel. Other indicators provided at the intersection may be one of these:

1. Pedestrian signage wherever there is an overpass to cross the road.
2. Distinct indicators of the movement of BRT buses that can be seen by the other lane users.
3. Synced indicators in the BRT corridors, which have dual pedestrian approaches to the stops (Pune Municipal Corporation 2016).

Intersections

At the design phase of the project, priority of movement among pedestrians, cyclists, other vehicles and BRT at the intersections has to be decided. Street parking is strictly prohibited for a distance of 50 meter from the intersection. Change in RoW and priority of movement is decided only at the intersections (Pune Municipal Corporation 2016). Design components of RoW in a 60 meter road are tabulated in Table 4.11. Figures 4.20 and 4.21 are BRT lane and station segments respectively. Figure 4.22 illustrates a 60 meter RoW.

Table 4.11 60 meter RoW

Elements of street	Type/composition
Footpath	Both side
Cycle Track	Both side
Carriageway	Two way, dividend, central BRT lane
Parallel parking	Yes
Street vending	Low demand

Source: (Pune Municipal Corporation 2016).

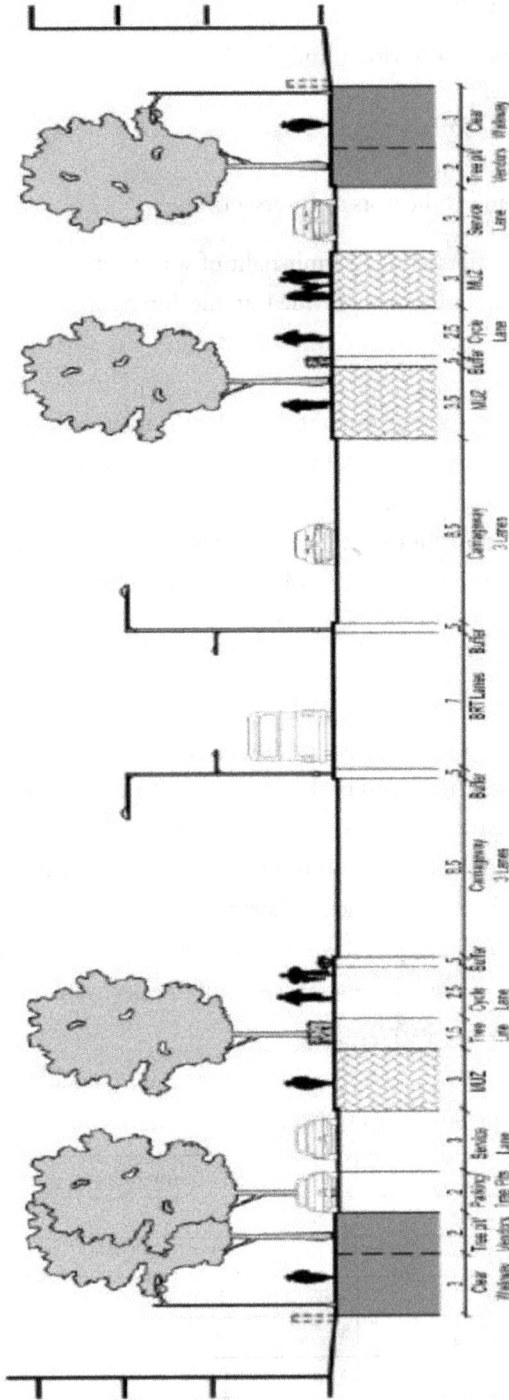

Figure 4.20 BRT lane segment

Source: (Pune Municipal Corporation 2016)

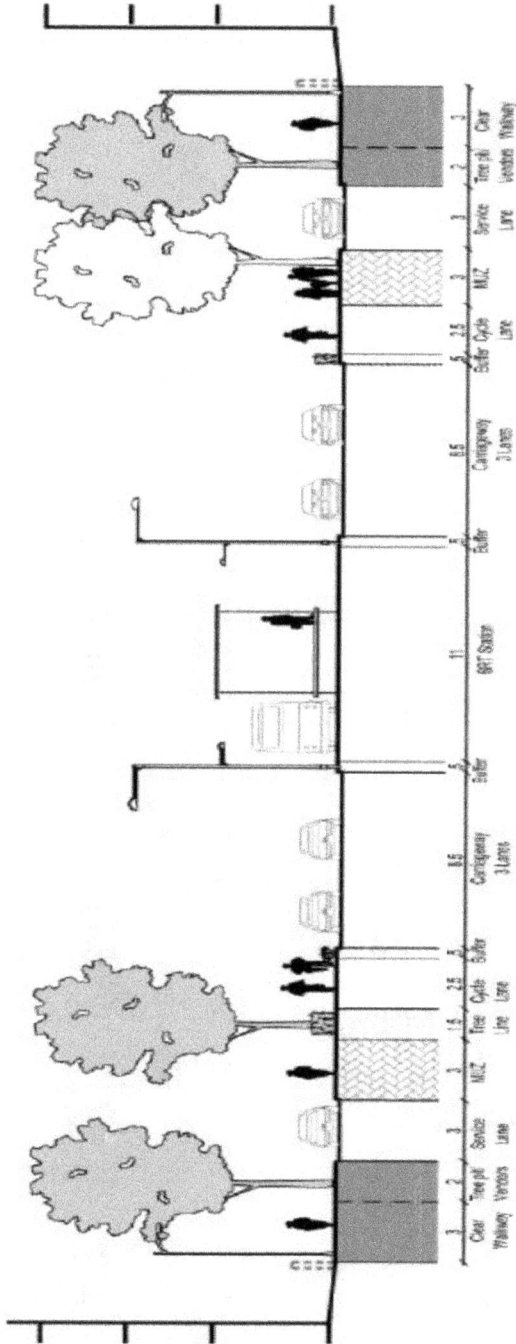

Figure 4.21 BRT station segment

Source: (Pune Municipal Corporation 2016)

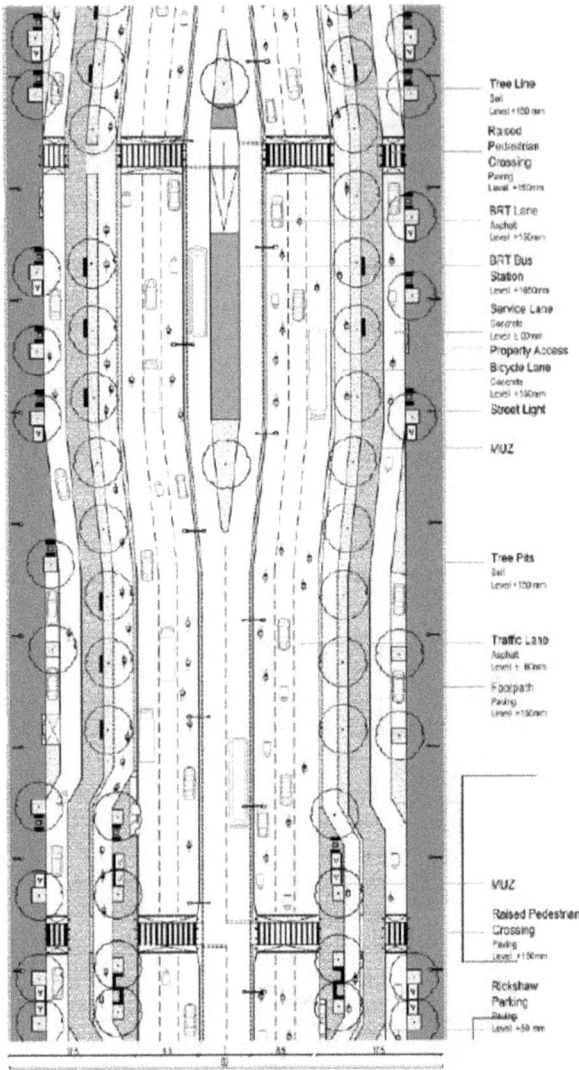

Figure 4.22 Cross section of 60 meter RoW

Source: Pune Municipal Corporation 2016.

Financial Strategy

The proposed strategy for fleet tallying was twofold. The primary aim was to increase the fleet size to meet the increasing demand. Subsequently, the aim was to improve the quality to such an extent that people would opt for public transport rather than personal vehicles. The broad goal is to reduce road congestion. (PMC, Detailed Project Report for Financial Assistance under MoUD Scheme for Purchase of Buses).

Capital Budget

PMPML authorities recommended that 1,011 buses be added to the existing fleet, the cost of which is given in Table 4.12. The total cost came to INR 39.53 million. Budgeting of ticketing equipment and aggregated cost for storehouse improvements are presented in Tables 4.13 and 4.14 respectively.

Infrastructure Provision

Ticket Vending Equipment

Storehouse Improvement Budget

Table 4.12 Aggregate charges for buses

Type of bus	Number	Cost/unit (Rs)	Total cost (INR million)
Mini bus CNG	111	2,500,000	277.5
Semi low floor—CNG (890 millimeter)	875	3,300,000	2,887.5
Articulated AC	15	12,500,000	187.5
Premium segment buses	10	10,000,000	100.00
Total excluding tax	1,011		3,452.5
Total including tax			3,953.1

Source: Bus funding DPR under MoUD scheme, Pune.

Table 4.13 Ticketing equipment budget

Item	Units required	Per unit cost	Total amount (million)
Handheld ticket machines considering 2.1 machines per bus	2,123	15,000	31.8

Source: Bus funding DPR under MoUD scheme, Pune.

Table 4.14 Aggregate costs for storehouse improvements

Cost abstract for developing a upper depot	
Project abstract	
Description of items	**Amount in million**
Buses parking	4.00
Staff/car/two wheeler parking	0.03
Boundary wall	2.61
Fire fighting	0.28
Watch towers	2.19
Sub total	33.07
Cost escalation on 2012 DSR (10%)	36.38
Electrical work @ 12% of total civil construction cost	4.37
Plumbing items cost @ 7% of total civil construction cost	2.55
Base cost	43.29
Non-core component	
Design, detailing and monitoring of projects during implementation, and so on (1%+2.5% of base cost)	1.51
Sub total	44.8
Non-core component	
Design, detailing and monitoring of projects during implementation and so on. (1%+2.5% of base cost)	1.51
Sub total	44.8
Project contingencies @3%	1.30
Total project cost (INR)	46.15

Source: Bus funding DPR under MoUD scheme, Pune.

Aggregate Budget of the Project

The collective ancillary costs with the storehouse improvement costs and ticket-vending equipment came up to INR 121.6 million. The estimated aggregate budget was INR 4,074.7 million. Project funding and budget for Pune BRTS is presented in Table 4.15 and breakdown of funds in terms of resource providers is presented in Table 4.16.

Funding

The MoUD project funding was through contribution of 50 percent by central authorities, 20 percent by state authorities the balance 30 percent

Table 4.15 Project funding and budget

Sr. No.	Details	Cost (in million)
1	Standard buses	3,165
2	Premium buses	287.5
3	Taxes (VAT 12.5% + 2% other tax)	500.6
4	Ancillary infrastructure	121.6
	Total	4.075

Source: Bus funding DPR under MoUD scheme, Pune.

by the ULB (PMC, Detailed Project Report for Financial Assistance under MoUD Scheme for Purchase of Buses).

Intelligent Transit Management System (ITMS)

Objectives

The PMC and PCMC with an objective to improve passenger satisfaction and loyalty in the BRT improved the management of the bus fleet. Intelligent transit management system (ITMS) was planned along with unified fare collection mechanisms and tracking of commuter statistics and monitoring of bus movements (Urban Mass Transit Company Limited November 2012).

ITMS

The primary objective of municipal transit was to alleviate road congestion and reduce toxic emissions. BRTS presented the option of achieving these at a cost lower than that of a light rail. BRTS offered more comfort and faster service to commuters compared to traditional transit systems. It incorporates modern ITS technologies to implement innovative and contextually relevant solutions for the (Urban Mass Transit Company Limited November 2012).

Benefits

ITMS offers a number of benefits to BRT. It helps in effective planning of operations, monitoring and controlling bus movements and tracking

Table 4.16 *Total funds breakdown*

Sr. No.	Means of funding	Grant % age			Amount (INR in million)			
		JNNURM	State	JNNURM	State	ULB	Total	
1	Standard buses	50.00%	20.00%	1,582.50	633.00	949.50	3,165.00
2	Premium buses	50.00%	30.00%	143.75	86.25	57.50	287.50
3	Taxes					500.61	500.61
4	Ancillary infrastructure	50.00%	20.00%	60.80	24.32	36.48	121.60
				1,787.05	743.57	1,544.09	4,074.71

Source: Bus funding DPR under MoUD scheme, Pune.

traveler statistics with minimum human intervention. Remote monitoring of bus locations ensures commuter safety (Urban Mass Transit Company Limited November 2012).

Resolution Summary

In line with the objectives of enhancing passenger satisfaction and loyalty in BRTS, ITMS was implemented to improve amenities to commuters and fare collection mechanisms. In addition, it also allowed them to computerize financial and operational aspects to enhance effectiveness and transparency. The additional advantages included reducing the travel time, better data analysis and communication with the drivers (Urban Mass Transit Company Limited November 2012). The ITMS fund allocation is presented in Table 4.17.

Master Proposal for BRTS, CIRT (March 2008)

CIRT proposed a master strategy of a unified network of BRTS with bicycle and walkway lanes with 21 corridors. The main features were coordination of existing practices, planned future developments, evaluation of NMT systems (bicycles), and available budget with phased expenditure.

BRTS, PCMC (March 2008)

PCMC proposed a comprehensive mobility scheme considering the viability studies of BRTS. Traffic flow studies and development of transit

Table 4.17 ITMS fund allocation

Sr. No.	Project component	Cost of DPR components (INR in million)
1	ITM system hardware	168.06
2	ITM system software	22.6
3	Contingencies (3%)	5.72
4	Administrative charges (0.5%)	0.95
Total		197.34

Source: Urban Mass Transit Company Limited, New Delhi (November 2012).

plans were incorporated in this scheme. Using data, BRTS was scrutinized for traffic flow along the corridors, the possibility of income generation and land space availability.

Summary: BRT Constituents

1. Dedicated RoW for rapid transit, punctuality of buses, and separation from other motorized vehicles.
2. At level implementation.
3. Computerized digital displays at stations and inside buses, including auditory broadcasts, to provide information about arrivals and departures.
4. Real-time monitoring and control.
5. Appropriate fare fixation and tracking ridership.
6. Unhindered entries and exits to the stops.

Promotions and Outreach Program (POP)

Introduction

Based on the analyses carried out by IBI and CEE, Pune, the customer perception on few quality parameters of the system was recorded and is presented in Table 4.18.

Table 4.18 Customer perception

Quality parameters	Customer perception
Passenger safety at intersections	Above 90% positive feedback was received
Bus frequency and fleet failures	More than 80% felt that BRT facilities were better than PMPML
Upkeep of BRT systems	More than 75% observed that BRT buses, RoW and commuter information were satisfactory
Congestion in motorized traffic lanes	More than 70% observed that BRT was economical and sustainable transit choice
Graded walkways for people with disabilities 40% found it satisfactory 60% found the lighting to be adequate	

Source: (IBI Group November 2016).

The POP initiative of IBI and CEE benefitted from technology advancements and effective project planning. The main focus was on the modal shifting of commuters from PMPML buses and personal motorized vehicles to the new BRTS. The developers considered timely and positive communication with commuters as a prime strategy for the success of the project.

Objectives

The POP proposed a design and implementation plan for PMC and PCMC. The objectives were:

- To incorporate characteristics that was critical for a vast section of society in BRTS as well as NMT.
- To gain the trust, loyalty and endorsement from the larger community.
- To earn acceptance, educate commuters and get their feedback.
- Customer engagement.
- Monitoring and assessing the efficiency of the transit system through POP (IBI Group, Shifts in Perception about Bus Rapid Transit in Pune November 2016).

Accomplishments

The main motto of the POP was to enable the municipalities in executing BRTS efficiently and effectively. The additional modules included signaling systems, customer feedback mechanisms and communication systems. A number of promotional activities were conducted in universities, community forums, through newspaper advertisements, social media and Internet about the BRTS.

Evaluation of POP

The effectiveness of the project execution was evaluated through:

- Customer reviews of promotional events and about BRTS
- An assessment of the situation before and after BRTS (IBI Group November 2016)

Assessment Approach

Determination

Assessment of the systems before and after the BRTS implementation helped the municipalities understand the extent to which the objectives had been achieved. In addition, this data also helped the municipalities formulate strategies for the future (IBI Group November 2016).

Timelines

The pre-assessment was in March 2015, Phase 1 was released in August 2015, Phase 2 in April 2016 while the post assessments for Phase 1 was carried out in November 2015 and for the Phase 2 corridor in August 2016 (IBI Group, November 2016).

Mechanisms

The community impact of BRT was assessed primarily through feedback. The basis of pre assessment was to understand the characteristics of BRT and its suitability for that particular geography. The design also considered the socio economic features of the communities living along the BRT corridor. The basis of post assessment was to evaluate the efficiency and effectiveness of the implementation of BRT. Figure 4.23 present the daily modes of travel prior and post implementation of BRTS in Pune.

Planning for the Future

Planning for the future was based on the prior assessment.

Commuter Acknowledgment of Rainbow BRT

Commuters understood that the BRT was both viable and cost effective. The pre assessment survey indicates that only 25 percent were aware of the BRT; this figure went up to 90 percent at the time of post assessment (IBI Group November 2016).

Daily modes of travel

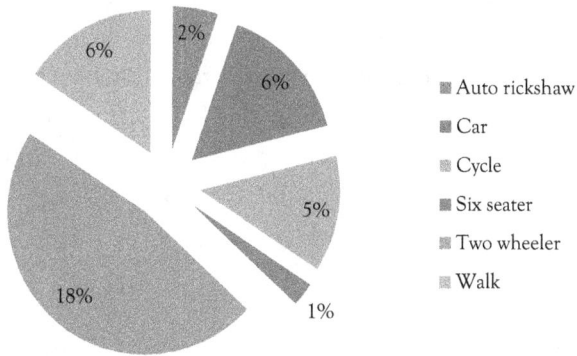

- Auto rickshaw
- Car
- Cycle
- Six seater
- Two wheeler
- Walk

Experienced the new BRT

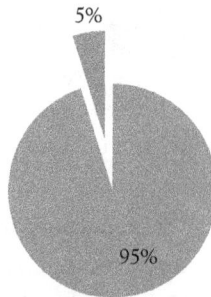

Figure 4.23 Modal stakes after BRT implementation, Pune

Source: Shifts in perception about BRT in Pune, CEE urban program, Pune.

At Grade Level of BRT and PMPML Buses

Commuters raided service quality, frequency of buses and display of information as important criteria for evaluating BRT. BRT was rated at 80 percent which was considerably higher than PMPML which indicates commuter satisfaction in terms of service quality and RoW (IBI Group November 2016).

Awareness Strategies

BRT used all media channels to engage with commuters, whereas traditional methods involved using only TV. Further, digital campaigning using web pages and social media helped in rapid dissemination of information thus creating a positive image for BRTS. For instance, in just three months, cinema broadcasts could reach 15 percent of the population (IBI Group November 2016)(IBI Group March 2016).

Land Usage

BRTS provided good connectivity to remote areas. This combined with poor parking spaces, motivated commuters to switch from personal vehicles to BRT. The post assessment indicated that around 40 percent of respondents observed that expansion of BRT was essential (IBI Group November 2016).

Events Blueprint

Framework

The project assessment framework included conferences by PMC and PMPML officials, NGOs, testimonials from stakeholders and feedback from the communities along the BRT corridor (IBI Group 2016).

The communication strategies focused on gathering data on BRT's performance and understanding trust building among commuters and their perception. The survey was conducted among the influential sections of society, organizational heads and diverse groups of potential customers (IBI Group 2016).

Outreach Techniques

Interactions with NGOs

Right from the beginning, BRTS had continuous interaction with NGOs and activists. The NGOs collected information regarding the difficulties faced by the communities and helped keep up the BRTS campaign effort. They visited the corridors to get the first-hand experience of the progress of the work and reported the problems identified such as the wellbeing of pedestrians and security issues at the BRT stops (IBI Group 2016).

Advertising Activities

Another dimension was to include diverse sections of the community that could possibly benefit from the BRT. Using a variety of promotional material, BRT was projected as a sociable, smart and affordable transit mechanism (IBI Group 2016).

School Assemblies

Since children have the ability to influence adults, the BRT campaign also targeted students. The positive features of BRT were communicated to them to help them understand the necessity of BRT in improving urban transit choices. They were also sensitized about the cause and effect of the current systems and the positive transformation that BRT might bring into the system. Campaigning was done in 17 schools across the corridors, addressing 1,781 student and 49 teachers (IBI Group 2016).

University Conferences

The conferences focused on the usefulness of BRT and also the NMT infrastructure. Graduate students agreed on the need for BRT in improving urban transit. However, they were critical about several operational details. One particular criticism was about other vehicular traffic having to travel a longer distance to take a U-turn because of dedicated BRT lanes (IBI Group 2016).

Community Outreach

Community programs were conducted in residential areas. Government officials also helped by facilitating a channel of communication between the communities and the BRTS; so that both positive and negative feedback of commuters reach the appropriate authority (IBI Group 2016).

BRT Campaign Inauguration

BRTS was projected as a system in continuous engagement with multiple stakeholders to plan, design, operate, offer administrative support and efficiently manage the urban transport system.

Free Rides

During the inaugural days of the BRTS, free rides were offered to commuters, along with promotional material that provided information about the BRT Facebook, web page, contact data, to get their feedback about what the BRTS offered (IBI Group 2016).

Broadcasting Campaign

The inauguration of the BRTS was advertised through the newspapers, radio jingles, Facebook messages and web page updates.

Challenges

Basic Features of BRTS

BRTS is a modern day urban transit mode with comparatively less capital investment than a metro. A typical BRTS would have the following:

1. Dedicated RoW in the corridors and for other motorized vehicles so that travel speed is optimized. However, the routes may not be continuous and around 57 percent may not have dedicated RoW. This space has to be shared among pedestrians, cyclists and other vehicles.
2. Off-board tariff collection as well as screening were not part of the design of Pune BRTs but were considered important.
3. Bus stations should have a provision for parking personal motorized vehicles nearby have suitable digital display to provide travel information to passengers. The bus stops were allowed to display advertisements to earn revenue.
4. The frequency of the buses should be planned based on the service quality, fares, and feeder routes. The small fleet size in the Pune BRTS remains a cause for concern.

5. Clean, well maintained buses, with a low floor facilitated ease of access.

6. BRTS planning should be rational, and able to cater to the needs of the city. However, in the Pune BRT, there was a huge gap between the DPR approved by the MoUD and the execution of the BRT. Adequate viability studies were not conducted before building the corridors. There were stretches of corridors that were much shorter than the typical distance covered by a commuter resulting in passenger dissatisfaction.

7. ITMS technologies can improve the quality by deciding transit priorities at the intersections.

Sub-Optimal Choices in Pune BRTS

Some of the reasons why commuters were not satisfied with the Pune BRTS are discussed as follows:

1. Delay in finalizing the DPR agreements led to poor utilization of the JnNURM resources.

2. The design was developed by PMC and PCMC in collaboration with IIT Delhi, which was not effective. However, the authorities continued to engage with IIT Delhi to procure the necessary funds, even though the documents were not intended to be used for the practical execution of the BRTS.

3. BRTS had no dedicated lanes for buses, bicycles and pedestrians along its entire stretch.

4. The cost estimates failed miserably; it rose from an INR 1 million estimate to almost INR 13 million.

5. PMC and PCMC failed to get community support for the BRTS. In contrast, NGOs were better at doing so.

6. There was no mid-course feedback and correction, and the authorities were also not willing to rectify any faults in the design and implementation, nor penalize those responsible (Nagrik and Sukhrani October 2013).

Limitations

The opening Phase 1 of BRT was a great achievement in being a first step in transforming the city transport. However, the following limitations were quite evident.

1. The bus-stops at the median of the roads made it difficult for people to cross the roads, and to board and alight from the buses.
2. There was a need for an additional four corridors which could not be built. PMPML need 700 supplemented buses but had to make do with just 350 buses.
3. The dedicated bus lanes at the median restricted the space available for the rest of the traffic causing congestion and overcrowding.
4. There was no uniformity between the heights of the shelters and the buses. Despite it being a pilot project, adequate training was not provided.
5. The corridor was not continuous throughout the length.
6. There was no room for bicycles, autos parking.

Summary

Other major issues were reported that were impediment to the success of Pune Rainbow BRTS and to improving the overall transport systems of PMC and PCMC.

1. Other vehicular traffic experienced unduly long waiting times at the intersections.
2. Bus breakdowns were frequent and station space was blocked by the inoperative buses.
3. Occupancy was very high during peak-hours and buses were over crowded.
4. Pedestrian jaywalking was common.
5. Other vehicles, especially two wheelers frequently used the BRT dedicated lanes.
6. Bicycle tracks were also often used by the two wheelers.

Such issues are mainly due to poor administration, arising out of lack of enforcement of rules and regulation. To overcome the long queuing of other vehicular traffic, signaling systems should be reprogrammed at each intersection and also should explore operating differential signaling durations for peak and non-peak hours. Mobile and fixed assets should be properly maintained so that breakdowns can be prevented. For reducing overcrowding, the traffic operators should consider increasing the frequency of services during peak hours. All other issues reported can be averted by strict enforcement of traffic rules.

References

Agarwal, P., A. Sharma, and A. Singh. 2010. "An Overview on Bus Rapid Transit System." *Journal of Engineering Research and Studies* 11.

IBI Group, C.U. 2016. *Promotions and Outreach Program for BRT & NMT in PCMC AREA.* PCMC: PCMC.

IBI Group, C.U. 2016. *Promotions and Outreach Program for BRT & PUNE Area.* Pune: PMC.

IBI Group, C.U. 2016. *Rainbow Bus Rapid Transit in Pune Promotions and Outreach Programme Events Report.* Pune: PMC.

IBI Group, C.U. March 2016. *Shifts in Public Perceptions about BRTS.* Pune: PMC.

IBI Group, C.U. November 2016. *Shifts in Perception About Bus Rapid Transit in Pune.* Pune: PMC.

Joshi, G. December 3–5, 2010. "Study on Travelers Characteristics and Reactions for Bus Rapid Transit Systems: Case Studies of Delhi and Pune." *Presentation.* New Delhi: Urban Mobility India.

Kathuria, A., M. Parida, C. Sekhar, and A. Sharma. 2016. *A Review of Bus Rapid Transit Implementation in India.* Cogent Engineering.

Kumavat, C., H. Sonawane, T. Patel, and A. Pansare. 2016 *Effective Learning from Delhi BRTS—A Case Study of Pune BRTS,* International Journal of Research in engineering and technology Volume: 05 Issue: 04 Pages 149-154.

Sukhrani, Q. October 2013. Nagrik Chetna Manch. https://mid-day.com/articles/pmc-should-withdraw-premature-fsi-proposal/15463178

Parate, M.U., and R. Shinde. 2016. "Transportation Management in Pune City." *IJSRSET,* 4.

PMC 2013, *Detailed Project Report for Financial Assistance Under MoUD Scheme for Purchase of Buses.* Pune: PMC.

PMC. November 2008. *Comprehensive Mobility Plan for Pune City.* Pune: PMC.

PMC PCMC. July 31, 2013. "Why BRT Right Solution." *Press Release*, p. 1.

Pune Municipal Corporation. 2016. *Urban Street Design Guidelines, Pune.* Pune: PMC.

Rainbow BRTS Text and Media for PMPML Website. April 18, 2015.

Rangarajan, A. January, 2010. "BRTS-Bus Rapid Transit System in Pune: Modeling, Simulation and Feasibility Analysis." *International Conference on Industrial Engineering and Operations Management, Dhaka, Bangladesh*, p. 5.

Rao, K. January 2011. *Evaluation of Development Plan Towards Sustainability for Pune Metropolitan Area.* Pune: PMC.

Jatar, N.C. July 9, 2012. "Public Transport System." *Paper for CDP-2041*, p. 11.

Savane, S 2016, "Bus Rapid Transit System in Pimpri Chinchwad." *Presentation.* PCMC: Pimpri Chinchwad Municipal Corporation.

Savane, S., and D. Jundhare. December 5, 2013. *Integration of Feeder Services with BRTS Corridor- Mumbai-Pune Road. New Delhi.* New Delhi, India: Presentation.

Transportation Systems Engineering Group, I.B. January 2014. *Road Safety Audit of Pilot BRTS Corridor at Pune.* Pune: Pune Municipal Corporation.

Urban Mass Transit Company Limited, N. D. November 2012. *Detailed Project Report for Implementation of Intelligent Transit Management System for Bus Rapid Transit System (BRTS), Pimpri Chinchwad.* PCMC: Pimpri Chinchwad Municipal Corporation, Maharashtra.

https://pcmcindia.gov.in/

CHAPTER 5

Conclusion

Urban Transportation

Urban transportation plays a vital role in the socio-economic development of a country. History has enough evidences of demonstrated economic growth based on high quality, superior access transportation network. There are also evidences of countries that failed to progress well, because of inferior transport infrastructure.

The motivation for a good transportation network has been manifold. Demand for mobility choices, specifically arises from a large aspiring and young population. Based on demography, young and aspiring population belongs to the developing countries and therefore public transportation projects are thriving in developing countries.

Motorization and technology (civil infrastructural construction, vehicular, communication and computational) advancements have contributed to improving the quality standards of public transport infrastructure and network. However, public transport development projects have not kept in pace with the increasing demands of the citizen, in most developing countries. Combined with the increased spending power, it has resulted in a proliferation of private vehicles, mainly two-wheelers and un-organized travel.[1]

---

[1] Auto-rickshaws are privately owned motorized vehicles. They are used for both personal usage and rental purposes, including plying school children. They are considered as an un-organized sector because regulatory and enforcement policies that are applicable on them are not clearly defined. This impacts routes operated, service times, applicable fare structures, ownership laws, safety and pollution norms majorly. They generally operate in short duration hauls as a cheap and convenient transport means, where public transport service quality is poor.

Government policies in urban planning and administration have a significant role in such public service management. At one end, there is on-going urbanization and agglomeration; also because of higher land prices in commercial centers, residential regions spread to urban peripheries, which increase everyday commuting distance. At the other end, governments are unable to provision mobility options at the pace of the demand changes and volume; the policies are also not unified enough to contain the private vehicle proliferation and to efficiently manage them.

Effectively, urban spaces are mostly congested and public inconvenience is prevalent. Increased number of vehicles on road pollutes the environment whose impact is more detrimental in the future. In the recent decades, World Bank has been pro-actively working with many countries to help protect the environment. Specifically related to public transportation, there are policy directives and recommendations on urban transportation. The global report on planning and design for sustainable urban mobility 2013 published by UN Human settlements program summarizes the physical characteristics of light rail transportation systems.

Impact Factors in India and China

There are several factors that are considered in urban transportation development. The focus of the discussions is on two of the fastest growing countries, India and China. The scale of the development activities is so large that the impact is global. The vital factors that contribute to urban transportation development are discussed in this section.

Modal Choice

Modern urban transport modes are metro, light rail transit (LRT) or the bus rapid transit (BRT).

Transport planners decide on a particular mode choice based on several criteria: some of the criteria are (1) population size, (2) population density, (3) land usage and spread, and (4) peak demands expressed in passenger per hour per direction (pphpd). Each modal choice has specific advantages and disadvantages based on physical characteristics which are presented in the Table 5.1.

Table 5.1 *Comparative discussion of physical characteristics of urban transit modes*

Component	Metro	Light rail	BRT
Running ways	Rail tracks	Rail tracks	Roadway
Right of way	Underground/elevated/at-grade	Usually at-grade-some applications elevated or underground (tunnel)	Usually at-grade-some applications elevated or underground (tunnel)
Segregation from the rest of the traffic	Total segregation (no interference)	Usually longitudinal segregation (at grade intersections)—some applications with full segregation	Usually longitudinal segregation (at grade intersections)—some applications with full segregation
Type of vehicles	Trains (multi-car)	Trains (two to three cars) or single cars	Buses
Type of propulsion	Electric	Electric (few applications diesel)	Usually internal combustion engine (diesel, CNG)—some applications with hybrid transmission (diesel/CNG-electric) or electric trolleybuses
Stations	Level boarding	Level boarding or stairs	Level boarding
Payment collection	Off-board	Usually off-board	Off-board
ICT	Signaling systems, Traveler information systems, advanced ticketing systems (magnetic/electronic cards)	Signaling systems, Traveler information systems, advanced ticketing systems (magnetic/electronic cards)	Signaling systems, Traveler information systems, advanced ticketing systems (magnetic/electronic cards)

(Continued)

Table 5.1 (Continued)

Component	Metro	Light rail	BRT
Service plan	Basic urban mobility with different classes of service with varying revenue generation	Basic urban mobility with different classes of service with varying revenue generation	Basic urban mobility with different classes of service with varying revenue generation
User Information	Clear sign board, route maps, real-time communication of arrival/departure	Clear sign board, route maps, real-time communication of arrival/departure	Clear sign board, route maps, real-time communication of arrival/departure
Public perception	Modern, state-of the art, comfortable	Modern, state-of the art, comfortable	More sophisticated than standard buses

Source: Adopted from the Global report on "Planning and design for sustainable urban mobility" published by UN Human settlements program (2013).

In the previous chapters in Volumes I and II, a detailed account of Ahmedabad BRTS, Delhi Metro, Pune BRTS, Singapore Metro and Yichang BRTS was presented. It is worthwhile to understand why these and other cities have adopted a particular mode. Other factors that influence an urban transportation planning are GDP, Per-capita income, road vehicle population, and so on.

The population growth over the years also impact on the urban transport systems. Specifically, one drives the other. When transport planners implement any transport system, the capacity to carry is decided based on existing population size as well as projected population growth. Many a times, economic development proliferates along the corridors because of efficient transportation systems. This in turn encourages more people to participate in the economic activities and therefore people use the transport corridors more frequently.

Population growth in the five cities (Ahmedabad, Delhi, Pune, Singapore, and Yichang) over last few years is illustrated in Figure 5.1. It is interesting to note that countries define urban space in their own terms and it may not be consistent. Around 2010 to 2011, China modified how it defines the urban space, and several cities those were rural earlier were reclassified as urban. One may observe that the sharp increase in the population of Yichang is because of the change in defining urban space.

Employment and GDP growth rate in the five cities (Ahmedabad, Delhi, Pune, Singapore, and Yichang) over 2014 to 2016 is illustrated in Figure 5.2.

The actual urban area (in square kilometers) and absolute change in GDP per capita during 2014 to 2016 is presented in Table 5.2.

Government policies also hugely impact transportation choices. Governments may attempt to promote public transportation ridership by favorable pricing schemes, user convenience and high quality of service. Mostly commuters perceive end mile connectivity, affordability and reliability of services as primary indicators of quality in developing countries. In developed countries and evolved societies, perception of quality may significantly change. Commuter perception is a vital factor and Yichang conducts very elaborate customer surveys, as presented in Volume II.

A comparative discussions based on the delivered features of the three modes are presented in Table 5.3.

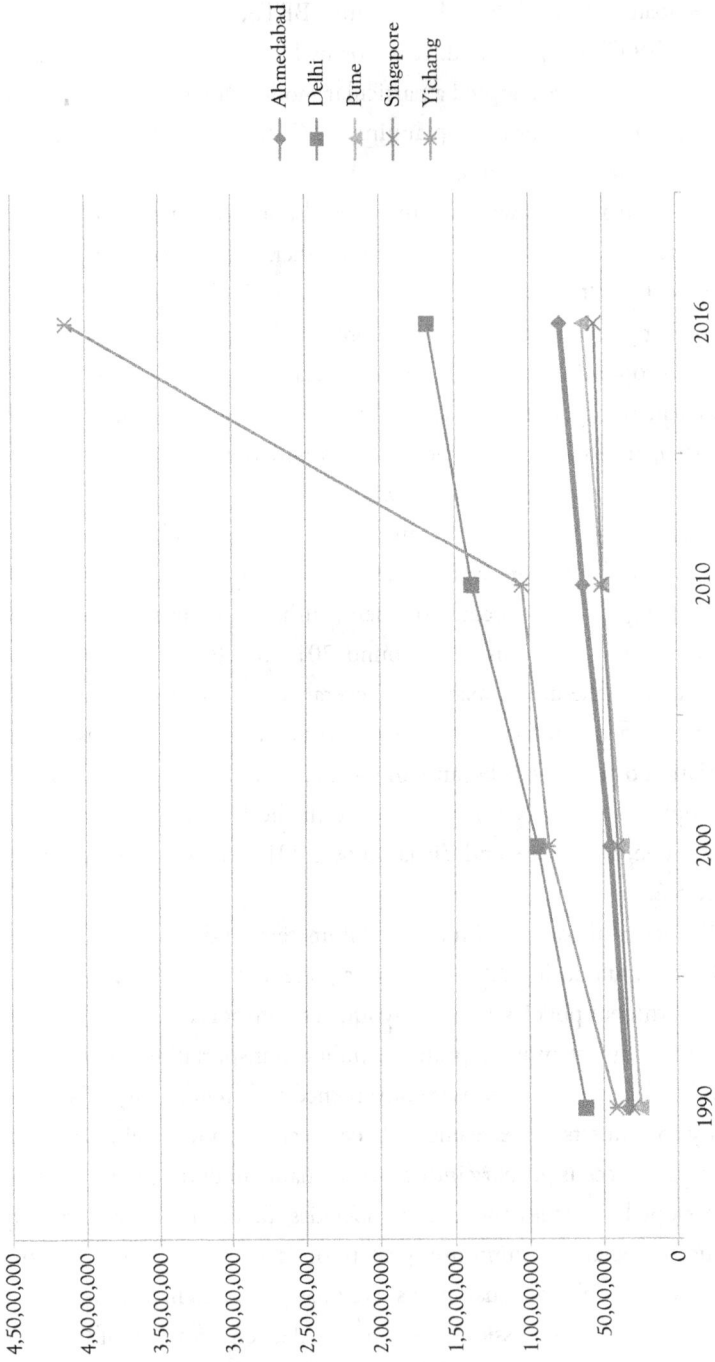

Figure 5.1 Population increase over last few years

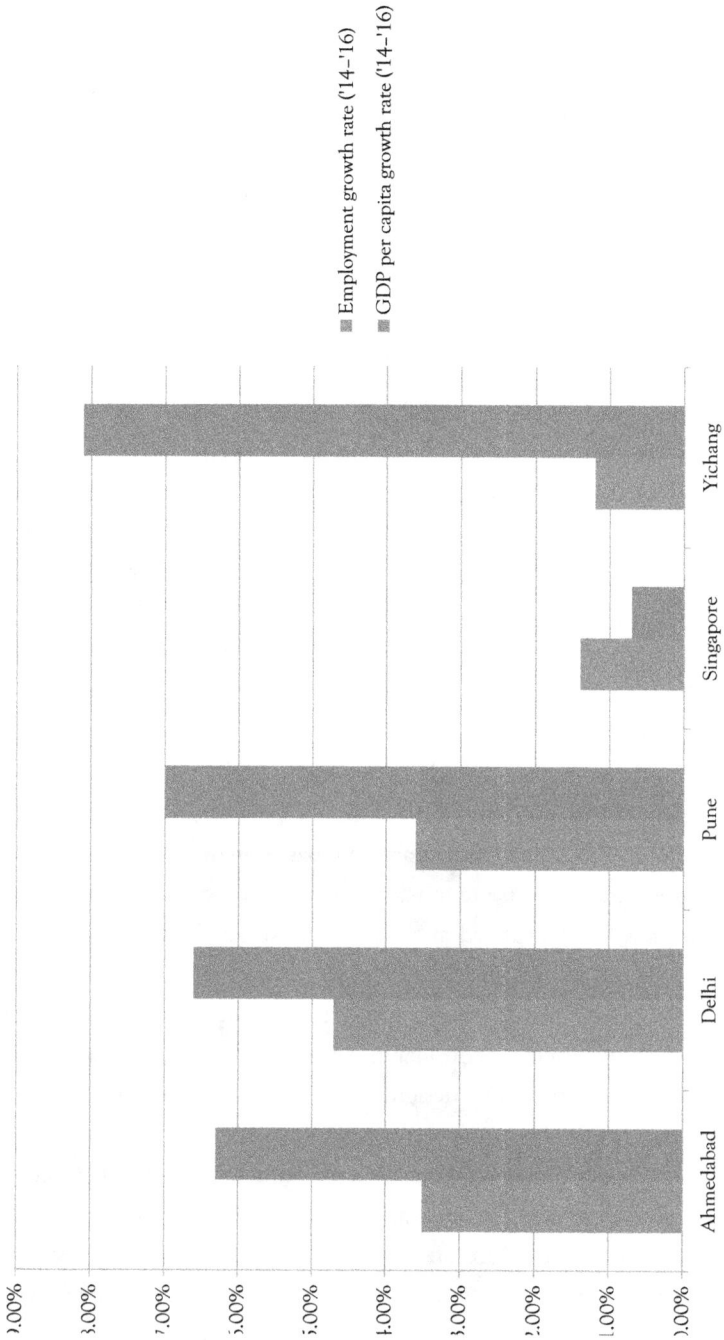

■ Employment growth rate ('14–'16)
■ GDP per capita growth rate ('14–'16)

Figure 5.2 Employment and GDP growth during 2014–2016

Table 5.2 Area and absolute change in GDP per capita

Name of city	Area (in square kilometers)	Absolute change in GDP per capita (US$), 2014–2016
Ahmedabad	471	+$386
Pune	276	+$530
Delhi	1,483	+$435
Singapore	704	+$689
Yichung	18,638	+$1,421

Conclusion

Summarily, there have been significant insights on urban transportation based on modern transport developments of all five cities discussed in the two volumes. Urban areas grow along with infrastructure development, especially related to transportation. As urban areas grow and develop along the corridors, there is a direct and positive impact on the economic growth, which is reflected in per capita income and GDP.

The basis on which cities decide on developing a particular mode choice is driven by multiple factors, including political reasons and development focus adopted by the government. It also influences the administration and commercial considerations adopted by a transport planner.

Several projects fail to fulfill the commercial aspects and many factors contribute to that. Many projects are built based on overly optimistic ridership forecasts. Forecasts are inherently error-prone and the error factor in forecasts is less considered at the planning stages. It is worthwhile to consider the economic impacts rather than financial impacts of a project; in fact, need ratification of several projects, particularly in Singapore, are confirmed using economic considerations. Cohesive policies are pertinent to effective project planning, design, development and operations.

Stakeholders in any transport system include citizens, government bodies, transport planners, system developers and vendors. For an effective implementation and adoption of any transport choice, all stake-holders' interests must be taken care of. This is one of the biggest challenges in planning and developing a transport system. Most often, stake-holders' objectives hugely conflict with each other's. How governments manage to buy-in their support and trust makes a big difference and the role of leadership is vital in earning public faith and trust.

Table 5.3 Delivered features of metro, light rail and BRT

Features	Metro	Light rail	BRT
Required roadway space	Low impact on existing roads	Two lanes (narrow 5–8 meters)	Two to four lanes existing roads (7–15 meters)
Required station space	Large reservation space, especially during construction	Medium reservation space (3–6 meters wide platforms)	Medium reservation space (4–8 meters wide platforms)
Distance between stations	Medium to high (1 kilometer or more)	Short to medium (400 meters or more)	Short to medium (400 meters or more)
Flexibility	Low (trains operate on fixed tracks)	Low (trains operate on fixed tracks)	High (buses can be used inside and outside the busways)
Traffic impacts during operation	Reduce congestion (does not interfere with surface level)	Variable (takes some space from traffic)	Variable (takes space, reduces traffic interference from buses)
Construction impacts	High (tunnel digging, elevated structures; longer time)	Low to medium (depending on type of construction)	Low to medium (depending on type of construction)
Potential to integrate with existing transport providers	Limited potential	Limited potential	Good potential
Maximum frequency	High (20–30 trains per hour)	High (20–30 trains per hour)	Very high (40–60 buses per hour per platform)
Reliability	High (no interference from other traffic, but could be affected by bunching)	Medium to high (depending on traffic interference)	Medium to high (depending on traffic interference and manual control)

(Continued)

Table 5.3 (Continued)

Features	Metro	Light rail	BRT
Human safety	Fully segregated from road users, low risk of accidents	Segregated from traffic only, some risk to other road users	Largely segregated from traffic, some risk to other road users
Air pollution	No tailpipe emissions, power generation pollutants dependent on energy source and technologies used	No tailpipe emissions, power generation pollutants dependent on energy source and technologies used	Tailpipe emissions for internal combustion engine, depends on the engine, fuel and emission control technology
Noise	Low (depending on insulation)	Low to medium (depending on tracks)	High (internal combustion engine and rubber-roadway)
Greenhouse gas emissions	68–38 grams per passenger—kilometer	100–38 grams per passenger—kilometer	204–28 grams per passenger—kilometer
Passenger experience	Smooth ride, high comfort (depending on occupancy)	Smooth ride, high comfort (depending on occupancy)	Irregular ride (sudden acceleration and braking), medium comfort (depending on occupancy)

Source: Global report on "Planning and design for sustainable urban mobility" published by UN Human settlements program (2013).

About the Author

Dr Sundaravalli Narayanaswami is on the faculty, Public Systems Group at IIM Ahmedabad, India. She earned her PhD in Industrial Engineering and Operations Research from IIT Bombay in India, after a Masters in Computer Science. Her teaching and research interests are mainly in Transportation Studies. Her scholarly articles on Urban transportation, Intelligent Transportation systems and transportation modelling are well published and read. She has a global professional experience; she was a fellow of the British Computer Society and she serves on the International Editorial board of the Annals of Management Science. She has an extensive consultancy experience, mainly with Government organizations in policy decisions related to transportation, technology and management. Dr Sundaravalli was the recipient of the *Distinguished Educator Award* of the IEOM Society International for the year 2018.

Index